YANKEE SANDINISTAS

Interviews with
North Americans
Living & Working
in the New
Nicaragua
by

Ron Ridenour

CURBSTONE PRESS

This publication was supported in part by The Connecticut Commission on the Arts, a State agency whose funds are recommended by the Governor and appropriated by the State Legislature and in part by contributions by numerous individuals.

Cover design by Stone Graphics

LC Number: 86-70942
ISBN: 0-915306-62-X (cloth)
ISBN: 0-915306-63-8 (paper)

distributed by
THE TALMAN COMPANY
150 Fifth Avenue
New York, NY 10011

CURBSTONE PRESS
321 Jackson Street, Willimantic, CT 06226

contents

Acknowledgements

Hundreds of interviews with United States and Nicaraguan citizens made this book possible. Moral support from Grethe Porsgaard, my wife, gave me strength at difficult moments. My friends Michael Roth and Michael Mogensen also contributed their advice and fraternity. To them, to the valiant people of Nicaragua, and to the internationalists born in the United States, I extend my warm appreciation.

FOREWORD

I first heard of Anastasio Somoza Debayle about the time I heard of Ngo Dinh Diem. Both emerged as Washington-controlled dictators, in my eyes, during the United States' quasi-invasion of Cuba. This patently illegal, unprovoked assault was launched on Cuba just as the new society initiated its campaign to teach all its people to read and write, much like the literacy campaign that Nicaragua would conduct two decades later. It was not until 17 years later, however, in 1978, that I found myself magnetically drawn to Nicaragua to cover the popular insurrection. I was not an Establishment "objective reporter," professing neutrality. Partisanship frees the journalist from those blinders to discover truth so that he/she may help turn evil into something good.

Ever since I met the Sandinistas, Nicaragua has held my heart, offering me one ray of hope for a potentially humane society in the future. In 1978, however, Nicaragua was falling apart. The faces of Somoza's soldiers were frightful to look at, and they knew it. I watched the frightened but determined faces of children carrying flags of the future and beating drums of sorrow for fallen friends. I listened to their stories.

I am of the philosophical school that contends human beings have two choices in this world. We either sit passively by watching history pass (today we may watch it on a wide-angle screen with our feet up on cushions), or we participate in events, in the "historical process," endeavoring to create a just society (or an unjust one, if one is greedy and power-hungry). As an angry American citizen I opted for participation. By 1979, I knew the United States would not be liberated in my lifetime (I am open to being disproved), something one of my interviewees, Sheyla Hirshon, speaks of in Chapter Three. Other people were fighting in unison, many were winning an opening. I, too wanted to participate before I died.

7

I got my chance when I traveled to Nicaragua in 1982, again as a foreign correspondent. I spoke with hundreds of the newly enlisted in what the Sandinistas call *poder popular* (popular power), and learned that "liberation" is not just a rhetorical political term. People were participating. They worked in the day and held meetings at night. They taught each other what they knew, and drank and danced, too.

In revolutionary Nicaragua, I met the Other Americans–Americans I could be proud of, even love. I met compañeros of the revolution, too, Nicaraguans full of life, full of hope. I traveled with a troupe of dancers and clowns to the front lines. There were bullets buzzing about sometimes, and sick stomachs. I shivered through attacks of vomiting dehydration, malaria, and who knows what all. A military doctor administered saline solutions and I went on.

Another time on a cooperative-run sugar refinery, I experienced something that left an indelible imprint on me. One day, I worked in the plant carpentry workshop planing a chunk of wood. Next to me stood Sergio-the-boxer, sawing boards freehand as straight as any electric machine. We chatted while we worked until the news came on the radio:

"They made me lie face down on Roberto. His neck was still bleeding where they had cut off his head," we heard an anguished agricultural worker tell a reporter.

Two recent graduate technicians had been ambushed on their way to a cooperative farm. Reagan's "brother freedom fighters" crossed the Honduran border to lay in wait for any random victim. They seized Roberto Alvaro and Dennis Rodriquez and cut off their living heads with bayonets provided by Uncle Sam. Before scurrying back to their refuge, these brave men halted an approaching vehicle with gunfire and forced those inside to touch their freshly murdered co-workers.

Sergio-the-boxer and I joined Alvaro's hometown neighbors later that afternoon. On the platform stood Alvaro's wrinkled mother. Next to her stood the agricultural minister, Jaime Wheelock. Our voices joined theirs as we sang the Sandinista hymn:

Onward we march companions
advancing the revolution
Our people are the owners of their history
architects of liberation

The children of Sandino
do not sell themselves or surrender
We fight against the YANKEE
enemy of humanity

The United States government had conjured an injured expression at this refrain and demanded a rewrite, which was not forthcoming. Nicaragua's Vice-President Sergio Ramírez explained instead just who the Yankees are and are not.

"The Yankees to which the Sandinista hymn refers are the ones who intervened in our country during this century, the ones who have impoverished our country, plundering our forests and mines...He is the Yankee who tried to circumvent the overthrow of the Somoza dictatorship, the same Yankee who now will not accept the fact of our triumphant revolution, and who arms, trains, and finances the Somoza guards, the counter-revolutionary bands; the one who supplies explosives to dynamite our factories and to assassinate our humblest workers.

"We are not, therefore, speaking of the working people of the United States, so frequently manipulated and deceived. We are not speaking of the Blacks, who have been humiliated and subjected to discrimination, nor of the thousands of Hispano-American immigrants. We are not speaking of ordinary North Americans, of their academic communities, of their students, of their conscientious intellectuals, of their labor unions that understand Latin America, nor are we speaking of those North American nuns and priests who have shed their blood in Guatemala, El Salvador, in the factories, in the countryside, in the universities. These are the people who can prevent a

Yankee intervention in Central America. These are the people who, together with the Vietnamese people, defeated the Yankee aggression in Vietnam. And now, demonstrating the great quality of their historical memory, we are sure that this people recalls its experience in Vietnam and will oppose with its entire strength a new imperialist adventure in Central America. It is up to these people to decide now whether they are going to have another Vietnam in their history or whether they are going to avoid this new Vietnam."

The ordinary U.S. citizen has basically accepted the role of passivity, has accepted not questioning the explanations for actions our government takes against other peoples, has accepted the so-called objective reporting of the multinational press, buying the American wisdom, "You can't fight city hall."

For me, it is the culture of resistance that must be promoted. It is not enough to portray the mentality, nor even the incomprehensible brutality of fascism and imperialism. The important thing is to show the example of those who resist–to show how we can resist together, and do so successfully. That is what I hope to contribute with this book.

The nine "Yankee Sandinistas," a term I coined, are people from the United States who live and work in Nicaragua, helping to create "el nuevo hombre" (the new person). To do so, they must by definition fight against their government's persistent policies of controlling other nations. They and their compañero Sandinistas are directed by love and hope. They have opened Nicaragua's warmth to many who would live a just life, an internationalist's existence. Nicaragua lights a candle for the future of our species. Do not blow it out.

Maria Hamlin de Zuniga, with daughter, Rebecca   *photo: Ron Ridenour*

Maria Hamlin de Zuniga

Health Care Is a Right For All

At age 15, Mary Hamlin began working as a laboratory assistant in the general hospital in her hometown, Minneapolis, Minnesota. Born in 1939, Mary had wanted to be a doctor as long as she could remember. Her father was a unionist mechanic, an admirer of the Minnesota Democratic Farm-Labor Party and Hubert Humphrey, the man who was almost president more than any other Vice-President in United States history. Mary took an active part in civil rights issues concerning Black people and Native Americans, many of whom lived near her. She was one of the first civilian Americans to witness the early stages of Wall Street's directed war against the Vietnamese people. In 1960, Mary traveled four months throughout Southeast Asia on a public health study project sponsored by the World Health Organization. I met Mary, now Maria Zuniga, 24 years later at a demonstration before the U.S. Embassy in Managua, Nicaragua. It was a familiar setting to us both. Hands Off Grenada was the rallying cry that day, one year after the October 25, 1983 U.S. invasion of the tiny island-nation. Maria was dressed as a Guatemalan native, people she had worked and lived with for six years. She and her daughter, Rebecca, represented their struggle for freedom. Others among the two hundred U.S. citizens gathered represented the fight for national liberation of other peoples. Nicaragua is Maria's fight today and her home as well.

When I was in Vietnam they were planning to assassinate Ngo Dinh Diem. I'd never been close to anything so tense. There were few Americans there then and we were conspicuously foreign. The first "military advisor" had recently been killed—déjà vu.

13

(The first American "advisor" pilots had just been shot down, September 1, 1984, in a northern town of Nicaragua, Santa Clara. They had strafed to death three little girls picking fruit.)

We could only go places with permission and then we were followed all the time by local military persons. Nevertheless, I learned a great deal. Most importantly I learned that major health problems of third world and poor people are not problems that depend on high technology curative care but require a change in the environment, a change in people's attitudes and habits that comes about with health education. I was exposed to a whole new way of looking at medicine from a public health viewpoint. When I presented my study to the Dean of the School of Public Health, he urged me to abandon my dream of becoming a doctor and work in the field of public health instead. There were, and still are, so few who come to realize the interconnection of all the causes of disease, that disease is not just biological. I had to make a very difficult decision when I graduated–go on to medical school or into public health. I decided on a two-year Masters in Public Health Education, which included another study of a third world culture, this time in New Mexico among Pueblo Indians. There, I began to learn about migrant workers, both Spanish-speaking and Native Americans.

In 1963 the federal government passed the Migrant Health Act, providing funds for the first time for health programs for migrant workers. My masters thesis was noted by the authorities responsible and they asked me to test out what I'd written about. So, I went from liberal Minnesota to Lubbock, Texas to work with Spanish-speaking migrant workers. Many anti-communist church and civic groups have their national headquarters there, and they claim the area is the nation's center of arch-conservatism. During the five years I worked there, I came into contact with the farm labor union. While such organizing fit right in with the health work I was doing, it was very dangerous in Lubbock. In my health work, as in my union-support work, I tried to have people understand the importance of organization. Health problems–like labor problems–are individual problems that require collective solutions. Medicine is very individual-directed; public health is community oriented. It is the community that is the patient. Contaminated water, diarrhea, gastro-intestinal infections, upper respiratory infections, skin infections are commonly found over the third world and in poverty-stricken communities in the United States. Where I was, the dogs on the rich cotton farms lived better than the workers, considered to be "only Mexicans."

Though critical, I still believed in the government's purported resolve to solve poverty related problems. It was my state's liberal Hubert Humphrey who introduced the Peace Corps program and he who interviewed me when I returned from Southeast Asia. When the Peace Corps began training people at Texas Tech University in community health development, my work had become known and the college staff asked me to participate in training volunteers on their way to Latin America to work among migrant workers. Peace Corps officials in Washington, D.C. then called me for interviews, which resulted in my coming to Nicaragua.

I worked up and down the Pacific Coast visiting sites to place Peace Corps volunteers, and supervising health projects. We also worked with the universities in order to give orientation to the volunteers on Nicaraguan culture. The contacts I made at the university for the educational programs were of *great* interest to the people at the U.S. Embassy. They wanted to know who my contacts and friends were and what they were doing. I was leery of this. With Nixon's election, changes were occuring in the Peace Corps. The Embassy considered the volunteers as part of the "country team." At U.S. Embassies, all the heads of departments belong to a team and meet with the ambassador every week. The Peace Corps head was supposed to be on the team, but there were only three of us setting up the program, so we took turns. I began to go and got familiar with the staff. They would ask me to inform about my relationships with people. Some of my friends were involved in organizing communities, cooperatives, literacy programs, doing consciousness raising. I belonged to a Christian base community working with couples and congregations for community improvement. Christian base communities work for the poor from the perspective that causes of poverty are not God-given, but that poverty has its roots in the exploitation and the evil use of power, exercised in this case by the Nicaraguan family government of Somoza.

Embassy personnel, and certain Nicaraguan politicians, told us that the opposition Frente Sandinista Liberación Nacional (FSLN) had existed at one time but had been entirely eliminated. A number of things happened about then to put that notion in question. In 1969, the lake flooded and Somoza created Open 3, a large area for the thousands left homeless. I helped with immediate relief for the flood victims, and conducted a census with university students. These people were simple survivors, living off the streets; almost none had regular jobs. When they were transferred out to Open 3–now a booming town called Sandino City–there was no infrastructure at all. The state didn't do much, so we helped out on our own time. It had nothing to do with my job as Peace Corps associate director. Because thousands of penniless people were just dumped in this extensive slum, there was, if you will, a "resurgence" of the Frente Sandinista. This was marked also by the assassination of Julio Buitrago, a known Sandinista leader who became the FSLN's first commandante, posthumously. He and a few others defended their safe house while 400 National Guard fired on it with tanks and airplanes. My office was just a few blocks away and I saw the tanks and soldiers. It was a state of seige. Afterwards, officials said a center of subversion had been destroyed, but I knew that Julio had died heroically combating the oppressive regime and done so in order that others, including Doris Tijerina, could escape. It was quite clear that the Frente was not dead.

Julio's courageous confrontation with this enormous repressive military body, and knowing how he cried out *Patria Libre o Morir*, made me think there must be some tremendous force that drives people to become revolutionaries. I admired

16

that courage to stand up. I saw that the only change possible here was a revolutionary one, an armed struggle. I had to do whatever it was in my power to do. I had some contact with Frente people, but I was in no position to take up arms; however, I could help people question and organize. You can't imagine, unless you've lived in a repressive state, how terribly, terribly all-encompassing that repression is. Most people live in constant fear. Even teachers fear the "ears" in their classes will report whatever they say, however they teach a subject. I knew I was watched. I was even followed while participating in milk distribution to make sure people got whatever was donated to them. The political officers at the U.S. Embassy wanted to know what we were doing, what people received what goods and services. One had to be very careful. Any mention of consciousness raising, of meeting with the poor for any reason was considered subversive and subject to repression, death.

Because of my refusal to be an informant, I had difficulty with the Embassy staff and the Peace Corps staff. At the end of my two year contract, I had to leave. The Peace Corps was only being supportive of a very repressive regime, and a time would come when changes would occur here.

Q. You met Somoza. What was he like?

An iceberg. He had no sense of even pretending to be charitable to the vast majority of citizens. To him they were merely beasts of burden. I remember a reception with him at one of his palaces. He put on a face of being nice, but you could see the hardness and insecurity in his eyes. Working with his cabinet members I was aware of the extreme corruption everywhere. Money would come into the country for specific aid programs–the flood, the earthquake–and the people didn't get it. Somoza and his cronies did. And I knew that the "political officers"–most were CIA agents–at the U.S. Embassy reported to Somoza, as they did to Washington, D.C. They were afraid of any efforts to organize people. Other Peace Corps staff did give information, often innocently. They'd be invited to fancy homes

17

for a big dinner, get drunk and give information about the communities and persons they worked with. The thing was I wasn't naive. I remember looking out a window of the U.S. Embassy, when a "political officer" was questioning me, and staring at Somoza's palace across Tiscapa lake. In the palace dungeon, a friend of mine was being tortured. How could I give information that could well lead to more of that? Being an American is not just one belief, one foreign policy. We must act for our rights and principles, or democracy is just an empty word.

Capuchin priests were acting. They were training staff members in 56 Zelaya villages. I had visited the Río Coco area twice as a Peace Corps volunteer and thought we should help out, but the authorities were against it. So, when I left the Corps I moved up along the Honduran border to work among Miskito Indians for a year. But the head of the program soon became ill and I took over the program, staying five years. I lived in a house once owned by a banana company. Later, I built a house on a creek two miles from Waspam village. I had three tiny rooms, a kitchen and a latrine in back. I had my own well, but no lights. I bathed and washed my clothes in the creek. The house lay on two acres of land with 70 pine trees. I planted lots of coconuts and fruit trees. I liked what I was doing. I wanted to work out the project, funded by Oxfam of England. It was interesting teaching people how to boil water for cleanliness, how to cure diarrhea. And then I met Marcelo. To earn money for schooling, Marcelo worked as a logistics assistant for the sister who had been in charge of the health program. I inherited him. He later became my husband. We speak Spanish together, but I learned some Miskito since it is Marcelo's native tongue.

I was living totally isolated from the rest of the country. There was no radio or television, only Voice of America, and usually no newspapers. I'd go into Managua three or four times a year, see people and try to catch up on what was happening. When I decided to marry in 1972, many city people thought that was impossible because Indians were savages. It was like being in a different country, but I didn't feel alienated. I was very happy. I could see the effects of my work: fewer people came to the clinics sick and I was carrying out "conscientization" in Zelaya as others were doing on the Pacific coast.

(Conscientization group dialogue for helping to develop social awareness was conceived by the Brazilian educator Paulo Freire. Conscientization, or awareness raising, has been adopted to health and nutrition work as well as to literacy campaigns in villages and communities, and practiced extensively in the new Nicaragua. Maria Zuniga explains in her contribution to a chapter of the Hesperian Foundation published book, Helping Health Workers Learn, *(by David Werner and Bill Bower) that at the start of the conscientization some groups will react negatively due to the fact that they are not used to this type of participation, but rather to simply listening to lectures. Some may ask the leader to "just tell" how things are. Others will see the process as a waste of time. The leader must guide the discussion to match the rhythm and speed of the group. People only fully grasp new ideas when dialogue leads them to act, observe, reflect, and once again act. When development of critical awareness is linked to meeting specific local needs, it can help people find the spirit, energy, and sense of direction required for effective action. A promoter's role must be as an organizer as well as that of a health expert. In Freire's approach, the educational process is open-ended and adventurous. Passing out information is considered less important than putting together the learners' own observations and experiences. To guard against manipulation or "brainwashing," Zuniga and the book's authors suggest the following for group leaders:*

> *—Ask questions that are truly open-ended without hinting at the "appropriate" reply.*
> *—For discussion starters use words, pictures, or objects that are familiar and will spark ideas.*
> *—Try to avoid stating your own opinions as much as possible or when doing so make it clear they are yours.*
> *—Be prepared for discussion to go in directions you*

19

didn't expect.
–Alert the group to your tendency to impose your own ideas on them.
–Welcome criticism and disagreement.
–Keep your language simple. Do not use jargon and cliches.)

This method of teaching empowers people, takes them away from fatalistic notions. Not everything is God-created. But many poor people never look at their own abilities. They just do the same things over and over again. Rulers encourage this because they want people to be ignorant, and thus powerless. Our hope was (and is) that people would learn they could gain power over their lives and unite with people throughout Nicaragua to change their circumstances. This is a liberating education practiced by North American Capuchins, Nicaraguan Catholics, Miskito Moravians. We integrated our philosophy with popular, social organizations for improving health and education, and political life. Eventually, people would come to Waspam authorities and say things like, "Why aren't teachers in the schools when they are supposed to be? We have a right to an education." This attitude change was considered subversive by officials, who sought to stop it.

You have to remember the whole area I worked in was the site of war games in 1960. There were many Indians who felt there had been a real war, and that the Yankees had come in to root out communists. The war games were, in fact, preparations for the Bay of Pigs invasion. There are still people convinced that there was a real war right in their villages. The U.S. troops "saved" them and left all sorts of nice goodies, too: food, clothing, equipment. The people didn't know anything about communism, but the authorities had filled people with fear. Communism was the devil incarnate.

By late 1974, the authorities stopped me from traveling up the river to do my health work. They just wouldn't let a plane in anymore, and I couldn't go by boat in my advanced state of pregnancy and with my other baby. The word got around that I was under house arrest. Then a National Guardsman told me I was a *persona non-grata* and would have to leave the country. I talked to a high official in the health ministry and we agreed the project was important to finish. So, I made a deal with them. They let me finish the project and then I had to leave Nicaragua and couldn't return. With the project's conclusion, I followed my husband to Guatemala, where he had gone to study in the veterinary school, the only one in Central America. Marcelo came from a very poor river family of 13 brothers and sisters. When he finished the first three grades in his community—the only schooling available—he took his little boat to another village to complete the next three grades. When he went to Guatemala it was his first trip outside Nicaragua.

Q. What was your relationship like with your in-laws?

They lived in a different village than we did and we didn't have much contact, but we had good relations. Sometimes one of their children would visit me. A ten-year-old brother of Marcelo's came to stay and he was absolutely intolerable. He never minded me. He was probably a typical boy, now that I have one. But I finally had to send him home. At our parting, I told him I hoped one day he'd turn out to be something. Well, he fought with the Frente Sandinista. Now, he's in Cuba studying on his fourth year of a scholarship, learning to be a foreman in a shop. The first time I saw him upon my return to Nicaragua he was dressed up in his uniform. I felt very proud of him.

The family member I got closest to is Marcelo's grandfather, Andrés. He had worked for the banana company and had had some exposure to different people. He was an interesting man. He loved to talk about the river and the "old days" when he'd been a cattle owner because he earned money from the foreign-owned companies. Most of his family, as most Miskitos, didn't earn cash. They bartered. I feel bad because when some of the Indians had to be dispersed from the river banks, he went with those who crossed into Honduras. I haven't seen him for years and I miss him a lot. It was through him that I gained acceptance with the whole family because he'd tell the others that I was alright. I never did have much problem because Miskitos have looked up to outsiders, especially English and Americans, and even think of them as better than themselves.

Q. That may be why someone as Anglo-looking as Steadman Fagoth Müller is looked up to by many Miskitos.

Humph. I don't want to talk about Steadman. I knew him to be a demagogue. I never felt that he represented the interests of the Indian people. I think he understood some of the legends the Indians have. You see, they believed one day they would be liberated from the Spanish, as they say. They see Somoza and Sandino as the same oppressor. They'd be given territory once again by the British Crown. Steadman heralded that legend because that gave him power over people. He and his promoters worked on that concept after the triumph through the MISURASATA organization. This legend isn't possible in the real world. Northeastern Zelaya is jungle and swamp and has very little resources for a nation. I was in Waspam the day Steadman was released from prison for subversion. It was by then known he'd been an agent for Somoza's security forces. He riled the Indians up, reminding them of their legend. He told them to rise up against the Sandinistas. I'd never seen them so affected by a charismatic person. The way he was talking was so Hitleresque that the person next to me said, "He sounds just like Hitler." And I said, "Hitler happens to be one of his heroes." I thought I was looking at some old film reel from Nazi Germany. Anyway, he left for Honduras to fight with the CIA and Somocistas.

Q. What did you do in Guatemala?

I continued my work training village health workers and promoters, using conscientization. After a devastating earthquake, in which we also lost our home, the government got even more repressive because of the volunteer programs, many funded by United States church and charity groups. The disappearances increased from scores to hundreds, then thousands. Religious workers were a prime target, as were labor leaders. The military authorities and the oligarchy were afraid the people would effectively demand an elected government, as they once had before the CIA backed its violent overthrow in 1954. I knew many of those murdered. Once I saw 15 bodies hanging from a tree. After the Sandinistan victory, peasants were killed in Guatemala at random. I stood up for the campesino demands and began having lots of problems. Peace Corps volunteers and all U.S. Embassy personnel were forbidden by Ambassador Frank Ortiz to have any contact with me. I continued to give witness and talk to whomever would listen. By 1980, conditions were so bad where I lived that I sent my children to the States. They were having nightmares of dying at the hands of the military. By then, my husband was finishing his internship. He had worked with farmers studying diseases in cattle. Two of the people he worked with were assassinated. He was warned he'd be next. Many people are told that they'll be killed. They sometimes have a choice to leave or stay and be killed. At the same time, they were following me. My husband graduated early and returned to Nicaragua to work with the new CIDCA (Center for Research and Documentation of the Atlantic Coast). I had to finish my work. I knew that once I left I'd never be able to return to Guatemala. Our family was reunited in July 1981. I was so excited to return to Nicaragua. I was met at the airport by Ernesto Cardenal who told me, "Welcome to your liberated country." I saw people I didn't know would be alive or dead. It was extremely emotional for me. Then, I met with the tragic reality that I wouldn't be able to return to my work and my life on the Río Coco. The counter-revolutionary situation was too dangerous for me there with my children. The CIA radio station, *15 de Septiembre* in Honduras, was already threatening my husband's life for the work he was doing. They would announce on the radio, "We know you're traveling on the river" on such and such day. "You are a traitor to the Miskito people. We are going to get you." We were told to live in Managua. Shortly thereafter, Waspam was no more. Everyone was resettled because of the Red Christmas invasion attempts. All I knew and loved, my home, my relatives, it is no more.

Between November 1981 and January 1982, Fagoth-led contras entered Zelaya territory from bases in Honduras, killing, kidnapping, raping, burning. Of the 60 people killed, many were Miskito farmers, hunters, fishers. Some, like Atim Chow, were found with their throats slit and eyes yanked out of their sockets. Because of these attacks, and the Red Christmas plan to seize Nicaragua territory in order to declare a "liberated nation" that would enable the United States to move directly into Nicaragua, the Sandinista government decided to relocate the Miskitos living along the banks of the Río Coco. Everyone was given a choice to move further into Nicaragua or cross into Honduras. About 8,000 agreed to evacuate while another 10,000 chose to cross into Honduras. No one died during the quick evacuation to new settlements in Tasba Prí. Nevertheless, Steadman Fagoth Müller, on an all-expense paid trip to the United States under the sponsorship of the ultra-conservative American Security Council, charged that 400 Miskitos had been murdered by Sandinistas, another 3,500 disappeared and the rest forced into "concentration camps." U.S. Ambassador to the United Nations Jeane Kirkpatrick even outdid Fagoth by declaring in a TV interview that 250,000 Miskitos had been herded into concentration camps. There are no more than 70,000 Miskitos in all of Nicaragua.

So, I did consultant work out of Managua. I made my health educational materials available to whomever could use them. Later, I went to work for the Ministry of Health in the central level, promoting popular education and communication. In June 1983, another health worker and I established *Centro de Informacíon de Servicios Salud* (CISAS), an information and advisory office for health personnel. We train people in methodology of popular health education. Students come from private, church and government agencies. They learn how to teach other health workers who relate directly to communities.

Our office is the only place that sells health educational material in Nicaragua. We have 160 titles from many countries in the Americas and Europe. We worked on a lot of the guidelines set up by the Ministry of Health used in teaching people how to create good health conditions in their communities. Our main task is to teach people, who are illiterate or nearly so, how to care for themselves. We seek to have a multiplier affect in any of our courses. Right now our projects include promotion of breast feeding, work with the women's organizations, and pesticide poisoning problems–Doug Murray's project (another internationalist from the U.S.)–and a slide show about popular participation in health for the grass roots organizations in Sandino City. Our next slide show will take on the abuse of drugs. People are brainwashed by drug companies, and they use medicines that are not good for them, or use medicines that may be good but in too great quantities.

If it weren't for the revolution we couldn't be doing popular health education. Not only can we do it, but we are encouraged and given help by the government ministries. Here, I am not a "subversive." Here, there is political will that people participate and create change for better health, for better lives. We just fit into a whole movement of building upon the dignity that the revolution confers on people.

But the costs are high. Our office is now working with the Ministry of Health on a document concerning the effects of counterrevolutionary aggression in the health sector. It is just astounding: 23 health workers killed, 22 health workers disappeared, 50 health units destroyed, 13 other centers closed down in the Zelaya area alone, construction stopped. Damage in the health sector runs at least $70 million dollars. The contras purposely terrorize people. They don't want people to have any of the benefits the revolution has produced and that includes improved health and education. They want to break people's confidence in the Sandinista government. They do create fear, but it is counterproductive because they also create a willingness to protect. People know the tactics of the contra are those of the dreaded past. They can have no confidence in that. It is the same in Guatemala and El Salvador. It is not the Sandinista army that slits the bellies of pregnant women. How can the people want to go with the contras? Instead, they want to defend the little bit they've gotten from the revolution. I'm sure that there are places where people are afraid now. But if you look at concrete examples of what happens in areas where the contras have attacked, you'll see more people signing up for the militia, for the patriotic military service, and in places where not many were for the Sandinistas before.

Q. Do you see this happening in Miskito areas?

What happened in Sumabila–one of many Tasba Prí settlements for Río Coco natives–was a qualitative jump in relations between Miskitos and the Sandinista government because when the contras attacked, the Miskito Indians defended *their* settlement. The April (1984) attack resulted in the death of many and the entire destruction of the infrastructure built by natives with government funds. That was the first time Miskitos defended the settlements in a massive way. Since then, Miskitos have fought back successfully in other settlements. And now there is much more communication and acceptance between Indians and the government. In fact, many Miskitos are now in the army and the FSLN party. It is important that the new native organization, MISITAN, is given credibility, visibility, authority. There are many very good people in the MISITAN. I know most of them. Mirna Cunningham and I have known each other since I first went to the Río Coco. Minerva Wilson and Hazel Lau Blanco were students of mine.

(Mirna Cunningham is a regional health director and doctor. She was kidnapped by Steadman Fagoth followers in December 1981, taken to Honduras, beaten and raped repeatedly with religious singing in the background, then released into Nicaragua as an example to others working with government programs. Minerva Wilson is a director of Tasba Prí and co-

founder of MISITAN. Hazel Lau Blanco is one of the two elected
FSLN legislators from northern Zelaya. All are Miskito Indians.)

For the first time in my life I am living in a country where the leadership of the country is truly concerned with the development of all the people, in seeing that the benefits from economic efforts are shared by everybody and not only enjoyed by a few. In the United States, as in Guatemala today and pre-revolutionary Nicaragua, we know that the profits of production only go to a few. In my own field of health, medical care is a right for all, and the participation of all is encouraged. It's important to me to live and work freely so that this philosophy can happen. I am willing to do all I can so that others can learn the truth of what is actually taking place here. People exercise a new dignity they so nobly fought for. Would we so fight to defend our family, our friends, our nation, if it were worth fighting for? The United States has never lived in a direct war situation. These people have. They know they want peace and they are willing to fight for peace.

Q. Why then is this government seen by so many in the U.S. as totalitarian, repressive, and communist?

This government is seen in that light because the leaders of the United States–supported by a multinational oriented news media–who have only their own material interests at heart and the economic interests of a few, are afraid that when people see what a poor country can do, that others will want to do the same, and even some in the U.S. may want to do the same. As more people live better around the world, those who have the most will have to give up–give back–a little. And that is what has happened here. None of the wealthy are poor today, but they may not have unrestricted license to do anything their money could once buy. If one person had ten houses, for instance, and weren't living in all of them, then some would be made available to those who have no house.

Q.What are your plans?

I would like to stay in Nicaragua. My plans are not to go anywhere else. I feel closer cultural ties with the people of Nicaragua and Latin American than the United States. In a way, I have been alienated from my own roots because people there live and think differently than I do. I've lived in volatile Central America for 16 years now and my own values have changed. Material goods are not important to me. I want to have food, housing, clothes, but not ten pairs of shoes. I don't want my children to develop consumer values. I find it overwhelming to go into a supermarket and have 15 different brands of breakfast food and try to figure out which one I should get. They sell them on the basis of a plastic car inside or something, not on how much nutritional value they may have. I want my children to be able to make choices on the usefulness of an item and not be forced to adopt false needs. People in the U.S. have unfathomable false needs.

Q. What will you do if the United States invades?

My mother is frightened that something may happen to me. Perhaps something will. But something is happening to thousands, millions of people. Those like me would be eliminated if the U.S. Marines come in. They won't be here to "save" us. They've killed so many already in country after country. But I'm not afraid. We can't afford to be afraid. The blood of martyrs actually does bring hope, hope that the revolution can't be destroyed no matter what the United States does. When I returned to Nicaragua from Guatemala, I met Donna Santos, the mother of Julio Buitrago. She is a main force behind the organization of Heroes and Martyrs. We became friends. I feel close to her because of the reflection that her son's death (and her own testimony as a mother of a revolutionary) created in me. She and Julio gave me strength. I want to be a mother like she has been. The revolution comes first because it is for all of us. If the revolution is destroyed, it will be far worse for my children. I hope they won't be taken in by the U.S. domineering consumerism culture. I maintain U.S. citizenship, though, primarily because it entitles me, and them, to go where I please. As a Nicaraguan citizen I'd lose much mobility and could be stopped from visiting the U.S. People in my position must reach as many U.S.A. folk as possible, just as we did during the Vietnam war years. As the U.S. elite squeeze the citizenry more and more, they become more open to learning, to rebelling. Part of the squeeze is the new so-called anti-terrorist laws. I got a letter just today from someone who said he couldn't represent a health program for Nicaragua in the United States. He was afraid he'd be subject to government harassment. I'm already known for my work, but others are not. This is my life's work.

Fred Royce   *photo: Peter Kelly*

Fred Royce

Putting Wrenches In Hands

Standing over a group of farmers, the thin, surfer-blond instructor gestures at the Caterpillar hydraulic-controlled contraption. The CAT is the only model available for instruction on how to maintain and repair the awaited shipment of 60 Yugoslav bulldozers, which are replacing the preferred but unobtainable CATS and John Deeres.

"A Deere is a tractor in Nicaragua. Anything else may or may not be," quips Fred, a tall, wholesome-looking 32-year-old man with piercing blue eyes.

Fred co-founded the Luis Hernandez Aguilar School of Agricultural Mechanization, along with Nicaraguan farmer Apolinar Altamirano Pichardo. Fred teaches classes and runs the garage, living on his salary of 5,000 cordobas ($180) a month in a narrow, duplex-type home. He has a marvelous view of the valley town from atop a hill in Matagalpa, a 20-minute motorcycle ride from the school, located eight kilometers from the nearest village of Sebaco. The trade school is the two-story brick house of a former Somoza senator, since confiscated by the State. It sits on six acres of farm land, surrounded by papaya, mango and citrus trees. Fred's two-dozen students are the most advanced of the 500 he has taught in three years here. They are employees of a large State farm company that plans to bulldoze stumps, make artificial lakes and build dikes for rice cultivation. Next to the Caterpillar part stands a charred, European farm truck. It was disabled, along with five others, by a marauding band of contras. They had recently attacked a farm six kilometers from Fred's isolated school.

Q. Do you feel in danger?

A little, yes. It would be clearly possible for a band to attack and destroy the school. They'd pay for it dearly, but they might do it anyway. The school is in a strategic site, no doubt.

Q. Would you shoot back?

Well, I'm not that good a shot, and I'd have to fight the Nicaraguan teachers and students to get at a weapon. But we all do vigilance night duty. I don't think the contra would assassinate me, even though State Security has told me twice that the contra is watching me. It would bring unwanted attention to their terrorism and CIA links. I'm not afraid, but it is wearing.

Otherwise, I feel great about my life. I'm privileged. True, there is a significant decline in an internationalist's standard of living, a certain amount of suffering. I've had hepatitis once, and maybe a little bit of it twice. I've had some severe flus. But I haven't had malaria yet. Sometimes, I have problems getting documents from official agencies. But the people are great. I could live here a long, long time. I probably won't do that because I value my existence in the United States. I am not an ex-patriot, and I love southerners. I can accomplish more there in some ways as a technical liaison person. That bridge is one I hope to build. I plan to stay at least until the school is solidly on its feet. I know I'll always be connected to Nicaragua. This is my niche.

(Born in Jacksonville, Florida, 1952, Fred Royce was partially raised by a Black woman, a worker for his mother and small businessman father. Although his parents took an interest in community activities and in school integration, he had no other Black associates. Sensitive, he asked why. Fred found his way into the anti-war movement as a student of marine biology at Stanford University. He was jailed twice for civil disobedience sit-ins. He left Stanford just before the administration expelled him, and worked in a warehouse, then drove a truck. Later, he attended San Jose College in northern California to learn heavy equipment operations. Between 1973 and 1975, Fred

traversed Central America. He visited Nicaragua soon after the 1972 earthquake. When he later heard about the Sandinistas, he remembered Nicaragua and thought the revolutionaries had a chance to win. He became involved with Chicano movement activities and Nicaraguan solidarity work. Unlike the image of the typical solidarity activist, Fred is realistic. More the horse-sense worker, he methodically went about preparing a new, useful life in Nicaragua. He worked for a CAT distributor, saving money and buying tools. As a mechanic, he could fend for himself wherever he was. He knew enough about underdevelopment to know Nicaragua could use diesel mechanics. Fred met Carmen, a Mexican student studying at Stanford. They married and immigrated to Nicaragua, October 1981. With their skills, they had a wide choice of jobs. Carmen took on administering the only higher education night school in Matagalpa province, and Fred's interviews with the Ministry of Agriculture landed him an immediate job preparing the new school for farmers' training in vehicle management. Three years later, he is indispensable to the school.)

I haven't made a lot of close Nicaraguan friends. The kind you go to their house for dinner. Some, but not like I would in the United States. I have more internationalist friends. We have more in common than we do with Nicas. But I never have negative experiences with Nicas. Well, one. The people doing development work want us, but those who give permission for residency, well, it's not always obvious to them. The whole area of planning is so inundated with foreigners who want to be internationalists. When we got here, we heard there were 4,000 working in Nicaragua. That's more than the technically trained Nicaraguans. I think that caused problems—not on a technical level—but in a sense of who was really running the show. And many of those who came were not always those best equipped to help the situation. Often the sympathizers are not the engineers but the psychologists, who are too much of a luxury here. Then it was also possible to control. A period followed when authorities limited the flow of internationalists, weeding some out. So, it took me two years to get official residency. I had to travel to Costa Rica every month so the Nicaraguan council could give me a visa stamp in order for me to stay in Nicaragua.

Carmen and I have little time left over after our work days, so we have a limited political or social life. We go to movies occasionally, the zoo, the Carlos Fonseca home town museum. There is some good ice cream here. We listen to radio, but not television. Most of the time we've lived here, it took a long time to prepare meals, in part, because we had no refrigerator. Now we have a one cubic-foot tiny fridge. Long periods pass without fresh milk, or cheese. Sometimes bread is scarce. Toilet paper is often unavailable. We eat beans, rice, some vegetables. Transportation is very difficult, although there are taxi collectives that most people can afford. I could never buy a car on my wage. The only thing I can spend my money on is a restaurant seafood meal.

Q. What do you do as a mechanics teacher?

I make sure the information the instructors teach is technically correct, and that it is presented in a simplified manner so people can understand it. Since some farmers still can't read and write adequately, these skills are also stressed, using hands-on training more than the traditional chalkboard. There are very few people in Nicaragua who have both a well-balanced technical education and hands-on experience. That middle-level technical worker usually doesn't have any technical background or school background. So the teachers one can draw from are either empirical workers who don't know how to read and write, or technically trained workers who have done something else as specialists. I filled a vaccuum, or let me say, I began to. My first co-workers were 16- or 17-year-old "mechanics" who had no experience. I found myself in the most undeveloped agricultural region and underdeveloped school in an undeveloped nation.

Before the revolution, the region had about 40 tractors and when they broke down, farmers made do by the skin of their teeth. They learned a lot of bad habits. Now, there are three times as many tractors. They come from France, Spain, the Soviet Union and Yugoslavia.

Q. How does the Soviet equipment compare with the American?

Half the price and more than half the quality. Nicaragua can't afford or can't rely on getting parts anymore for American equipment. So, they get a good deal with the eastern models.

In a practical sense, I show people how to maintain these farm vehicles, as well as make sure that drivers get a good appreciation of the damage they can do, the reasons behind basic maintenance, good operating procedures. There were no prepared materials, so I designed my own. I have to put wrenches in people's hands. Many have never even handled a wrench, and none own cars. They can do wonders with a machete, but they have never honestly ever seen a wrench. It's unreal.

It is hard for the students to take on new habits. One of our problems is how to transform something, writing down on paper what work we are gonna be doing, and then doing it. Like a check list for servicing a machine, keeping a record of work in progress. That whole concept is very alien to them. If I were to go away, it wouldn't be a day or two before it wouldn't get done. They get to a certain point then drift off. To fix responsibility is a big problem. One of the reasons for lack of follow-through has been hundreds and hundreds of years of not knowing how to read and write. All they know comes from empirical experience. Nicaraguans are tactile people–valid and valuable–but often the senses are not accurate, and when it comes to machines one must be accurate.

The new methods I introduce meet with no resistence. Nobody thinks they are bad ideas. That's part of the revolutionary experience, realizing that the past ways of doing things are suspect. Underdevelopment is suspect, and rejected. Unlike most societies, the standard refrain of "Well, that's the way we've always done it," doesn't count here. Sometimes it's an explanation, but not an excuse, and that is nice, real nice.

I can honestly say that these men are still full of enthusiasm, five years after the victory. Their will to learn is more than an average teacher in the United States can imagine. They work long hours and some study regularly afterward. Then there's always some kind of meeting, or a political class in the evenings. Plus nightly vigilance patrols. But their work habits, well, I must say, it is mostly spasmodic. Nicas are best at the worst moments, in crisis times. Let anybody attack and they are all Johnny-on-the-spot. But they lack discipline, consistency. There are historic reasons for this. A cultural characteristic coming straight out of colonial domination is a lack of self-confidence to communicate. To survive hundreds of years of inherited domination and oppression, folk acquired a humbleness and a steeling of nerves, a clamming up. Looking up, questioning, is asking for trouble.

Q. What do the community people, the farmers, think of the school, and of you?

The school has come to represent the enormous possibilities for humanitarian cooperation between the people of the United States and the people of Nicaragua. Nicaraguans view me as an authority on almost anything because I'm a foreigner, and because they have come to view foreigners as more powerful, more competent, which leads many to a state of self-denigration. Now, they are breaking out of this colonial-imposed notion. Foreigners have been the masters of development, but it is not a necessity, nor will it be the only reality any longer. As internationalists, we must be aware that people often defer to foreigners, without meaning it they accept what we say. It may just mean they aren't gonna argue with you.

The difference between an internationalist and a foreigner is that an internationalist has more duties and rights. A foreigner could be a tourist or a business person, somebody not

36

evidently committed to moving Nicaragua ahead. An internationalist is committed to improving the lot of Nicaraguans and as such becomes involved in some decision-making and the daily life in whatever institution he/she is working at. I can be effective because of the tremendous acceptance Nicaraguans have for internationalists, an openness and lack of prejudgement that amazes me in a country that is under brutal attack by the government of my country. It goes beyond those I work with. I meet this warm, accepting attitude on the streets, among campesinos, soldiers, the police. A lot of Nicas see me–see us–in a positive way, which is the way I try to look at it, too–"That son-of-a-bitch doesn't have to be here, but he is. He may not be here tomorrow, but by God he is here today, and that's something." Why people get involved in things is not always clear.

Q. How is your school financed?

All the tools and much of the money and heavy equipment comes from donations from individuals and institutions in the United States. CAPP Street Foundation in San Francisco has donated thousands in tuition money and tools for student-workers. The Presbyterian Hunger Program and the Fund for Tomorrow donate many items: a lathe, a milling machine, a steam-cleaner. The Nicaraguan Ministry of Agriculture pays the salaries for the teachers, a kitchen worker, and subsidizes student classes.

Project Breaking Ground is an effort we began in January 1983 with the object of seeking understanding of the revolution and funds for tools. I travel to U.S. cities with the project, showing slides and giving talks. There, as well as here, I meet with politicians, clergy, solidarity workers, reporters, anyone interested in learning what we do. In one North Carolina meeting, right in the home territory of Senator Jessie Helms–one of Nicaragua's arch enemies–a farmer donated a two-ton chain hoist after seeing slides of students lifting heavy machinery with a lever and muscle. On another trip, I brought back a diesel motor, an electric pump and many hand tools.

The first group of North American farmers just came through Nicaragua to observe the revolution and the mixed forms of farming: private landowners, cooperatives, and State collectives. They left a gunny sack full of wrenches and sockets, tape, vice-grips, and odds and ends. They came from California, Wisconsin and South Carolina, about 20 in all. At the end of their tour, they held a press conference praising the progress they've seen here. They said that upon their return, they would work to broaden support among farmers.

We just signed a $40,000 contract with CAPP Street to train our first group of 50 private cooperative farmers. A great part of this program is that the students will get to keep the tools they'll be supplied with. Project Breaking Ground has raised perhaps as much as $100,000, much of it in tool donations.

Aid that comes from the United States is more appreciated than Americans might believe. It helps Nicaraguans believe that the American people in Yankee land are not their enemy. People tend to make a real clear distinction between the U.S. government policy and the American people themselves.

I believe that by writing off Nicaragua's revolution, the United States government is allowing Cuban and Soviet solidarity workers to gain an ideological upper hand in the minds of more and more Nicaraguans. They see these internationalists and the technology they bring and not the long historical conflicts. The United States talks about democracy and what have you, but it seems to many that it is just talk. Where was the democracy under Somoza, when the U.S. was quite content with that government for 40 years, and not a breath of democracy? But now all of a sudden, democracy is what's important, and that is what "we" are fighting for now by promoting contra torturers.

Q. How do you compare Nicaragua today with what you saw in 1974?

I saw more hunger and misery than I saw anywhere in Central America when I was first here. And there were these swaggering, smug-faced soldiers everywhere. People in this rural town where I stayed, San Carlos, warned me to stay away from them. The people didn't know me but they had enough concern to see that I was young and evidently out of my element. They hated the national guard and Somoza, yet most had a picture of him on their dirt-walled huts. It was safer to have his face on display. Someone, who also didn't know me, wasn't so kind. In a drunken stupor, he tried to kill me by pistol-whipping me. His son stopped him in time. This sort of thing happened a lot. Impersonal, yet very personal, violence right out of a wild west picture show. They wore boots, cowboy hats, pistols, rode horses, and shot at each other. People who didn't have pistols or horses, did it with machetes on foot. Since the revolution, that personal violence has declined greatly. On another level, violence of soldiers against the population has stopped. The national guard continues their brutal treatment, but now as counterrevolutionaries. Just two weeks ago, we were attacked close by. About 300 contras killed a few militia defenders. A major farm producer was captured, too. Seems he refused to cooperate. They wanted his land for refuge and demanded he stop producing. They took him from his farm and cut him in pieces alive. They stuffed his parts in a sack and left it on his property.

Sandinista soldiers are decent people. They make mistakes, and occasionally a drunken soldier shoots accidentally or stupidly, but they are arrested and punished for such behavior. More people have guns now, what with the war and civil defense, but there are more sobering attitudes toward weapons. And there is no longer the endemic frustration that decision-makers are untouchable. Now, there are recourses, and you can scream at authorities without fear of reprisals.

What impresses me most about the revolution is its openness, its willingness to listen, to explore. If the United States is ever as threatened as is Nicaragua today, I would hope that we could be as open, as accepting, as self-critical and as democratic as the Nicas are. Unfortunately, I have my doubts. We are seeing something here that for me is an example of how big people can be under real, real tough circumstances. I'm gradually becoming aware of what it means on an individual, community and national level to stand up to the United States. It takes a lot of fortitude, and not everybody in Nicaragua is up to it. You can find people here who'll tell you they hope the marines invade. These people were better off before the revolution. They have no stomach for an independent Nicaragua. Between that extreme and the people who defend and love the revolution, are people who vacillate, who waver in the face of the tremendous undertaking unfolding. Aside from the vacillators and the people who have just caved in, most of the people are willing to do whatever is necessary to gain national independence, which they believe is necessary to form a just, democratic society.

Q. The costs are extremely high, and the U.S. could buy such a small nation off, as it has Grenada. Why do Nicaraguans resist?

Dignity. I can think of no other explanation, except dignity, for what motivates people to suffer as they do. The contras kill to wrench away the country again. The United States government means to exterminate these people who dare to lift themselves out of that terrible thing known as under-development, a condition sort of like slavery where one's labor is not free but darn close to it, where one barely maintains existence, hardly any hope—an existence without reason, without future, something nobody should have to suffer, and yet the United States of America threatens with extinction people who try to break out of that misery. Dignity, and automatic weapons, is the best defense Nicaragua has.

It looks to me like we are getting something done here that's important not only to Nicaragua but important to many countries that find themselves in a similar situation. It is, in fact, a good example. Perhaps, being the example it is—a road to independent and fruitful economic, cultural, social well-being—is why the United States fears Nicaragua. It's an example the United States' power elite did not create and does not control, and therefore something to be destroyed.

Q. The U.S. poses the revolution as totalitarian, and the elections as a communist farce. What do you say?

Well, that's why I am here, why we internationalists are here, to do what we can to correct those lies and distortions. Why I am here is not always so tangible to folks back home. The concept that most Americans have of why anyone like me would work here is a get-rich-quick scheme. Some I know say about my working here that "Nicaragua must pay pretty good." On a very basic level I do get paid very well. I get paid by being part of a social process, a work process, where people are really pulling together to get something done that is worth doing on a very human level. Most Americans don't find that when they meet others like themselves in their churches or union halls. To Americans, struggling to break out of the bottomless pit of colonialism and underdevelopment is just unacceptable. On a kind of vague level, any necessarily social means to win power over one's life is just unpalatable to Americans. I wish Americans could be proud of Nicaraguans. After all, the good guy wins here. Nicaraguans are the people who took back their country, and they did it against a no-holds-barred war. And now they must confront another, even bigger war against nearly hopeless odds, one guided by the world's mightiest military power.

(The next time I visited Fred was during the last week of the heated election campaign. Daniel Ortega was coming to Matagalpa for a rally of 10,000 people. Entering Fred's home, I rushed past three young Nicas collecting paper hats imprinted with the insignias: Seguimos con El Frente [Forward with The Front–FSLN], and headed toward the latrine, diarrhea demanding discharge. Afterwards, I used a bucket of rain water collected from the slanted rook to wash down the defecation. The house has no running water.

Besides Fred and Carmen, and a young Nicaraguan adult school teacher, another North American internationalist lives periodically in the narrow four-room unit. Sheryl Hirshon, known as Sheyla in Latin America, is expected in from the "boondocks" for the eventful rally. Sheyla spends weeks on end in northern Matagalpa coordinating adult education.

Fred has taken a seat on the floor by the door as it rains in, splashing his pant bottoms bunched up around work-worn shoes, an indication of his permanent weight loss since buying them in Florida.)

Carmen's gone. I don't think she's coming back. The revolution, Nicaragua, is our problem. She thinks I'm more dedicated to the revolution, to a 16-hour work day, than to family stability. After three years of living with a phantom, she got fed up. I just got a letter from her yesterday. She's decided to stay in her Mexican hometown.

When we first came here, we were very close. I didn't know then I'd stay so long, but I pitched right in. I couldn't know how effective I could be. Being both a U.S. citizen as well as a mechanic has a certain practical as well as news value. Given my capabilities for advancing the revolution—helping in concrete ways to maybe curtail the damage the United States government does—I just don't feel it would be correct to leave Nicaragua. Nor would it work out to have children when it would compromise my work. But Carmen was in a different position. She was of little news value, felt out of her element in this tumultuous, often inefficient, revolution, in which she had "neither voice nor vote." In Mexico, she has both. I'll miss her. But she seems happy there...

Hey, I haven't told you about our snake. We got a boa at school. He looks brave, but that's for show. It's his only defense. Boas can't run fast and they can't fly away. I grab his head everyday; anybody can pick 'em up. A campesino brought him in, lured by the 50 cordobas per foot that I'm paying for boa constrictors. I'm protecting them from the Nicaraguans. The peasants automatically kill a boa when they find them. It's a macho-hunter attitude. There's another snake around here that's big and very poisonous. They don't kill them. They're so afraid of them that they run like hell when they see them. Many'll tell me they think a boa is poisonous at night but not at day, so they kill 'em in the day time. Boa constrictors have no interest in wrapping around people. Our boa won't even wrap around a damn oppossum because he thinks it's too big to eat. It can judge by looking at it whether it can get its mouth around it and swallow it. A boa is sensible. It won't kill anything it can't eat. They are completely harmless, not aggressive at all, and they kill a lot of vermin. So, apart from being a harmless creature in nature that people shouldn't kill, the boa is also a beneficial animal to man. So, I'm offering money for 'em so they'll catch 'em and not kill 'em, and so, if we can tame him, the school will have a mascot. Then, when campesinos come by, they can see boas are alright and maybe won't kill them.

Q. Can you let the boa run loose?

Darn tooting. He runs around the office and eats rats, but he won't touch a bat. Unfortunately, the other day he hid and we couldn't find him. The secretary pulled out a book that was in the wrong place in the library, and a head popped out with its mouth open, hissing at her. She almost fainted. And the tears! Oh, it was bad. So, we had to quarantine the poor snake to his box until she recovers.

Q. I have recently eaten at a café run by an obviously homosexual person. No one seemed affected by his gay behavior. I've noticed several artists are gay as well. Do you have any notion of how Nicaraguans approach homosexuality?

Our first group of tractor students contained an apparent gay, Bernardo, who went through the course with flying colors, in a certain sense. But he didn't like to drive tractors, which is a certain disadvantage in a tractor-driving school. Now, Bernardo didn't get real shit from the others, just some verbal harassment

43

and a certain ostracism. Living close together, maybe 25 in one room, doesn't provide much privacy, and they make a lot of sexual jokes. No weird stuff happened with him, though. Thank God. But he was referred to often as a woman. I don't think it would be a picnic to be a gay here, but they aren't beaten or jailed.

Come time for student evaluations, the Nicaraguans involved were convinced this guy wasn't gonna work out as a driver and, in fact, ought to be just disregarded in the future mechanization of the countryside. The school's three internationalists—a Venezuelan, Argentinian and me—expressed our liberal opinions about gays as no less suitable, etc. The Nicas were really listening like they hadn't heard this before. And so we took it on. We were gonna find a place for Bernardo. He was sent to a little isolated farm, fairly heavily mechanized. He stayed there for over a year, under very difficult conditions, conditions I don't know if I could handle for more than a week. He kept the records on all the different aspects of tractor operations. They were probably the best records kept in the whole region. Now since then, he's gone on and had a variety of jobs, and recently I heard he was offered an incredibly high salary, 9,000 cordobas a month, to do quality control. He is still different, but he is allowed, even encouraged, to do his work.

Q. What is your vision of Nicaragua's future?

Of course, it's possible there will be one horrible holocaust. The people know it. They ask me if I plan to be here for the second reconstruction, which they say will be a lot worse than the first one that left 50,000 dead. People have no illusion about what the United States can do if Reagan is left to his own wishes. Yet there is not a fatalistic pall. It's kind of funny. People who usually believe the U.S. will certainly invade, periodically tell me they just recently concluded it won't. They seek signs for encouragement. And, of course, nobody thinks anymore that the Soviets will or can prevent a full-scale U.S. invasion. They think international solidarity helps, especially from the west, but it is not possible for any other nation to defend Nicaragua. So, against all logic, there is an optimism that things will turn out all right. It is not a heady, silly optimism, but a kind of minimal, necessary, survival optimism—an attitude to push ahead despite the fact that everything will be torn down in a full-scale war.

If that doesn't happen, then their future is much more positive than the rest of Central America. Even now with high prices and inflation, Nicaragua has less inflation than the rest of Central America, all of it under the direction and control of Dollars USA. The steps the revolutionaries have taken to invest in long-term production, in a diversified economy, instead of luxury-living-now is the basis for a future sound economy. The whole election effort lays a firm political basis for an authentic pluralistic society, more so than most other nations. The willingness to open their country to the whole world, to accept help and criticism does them great credit. Nor does it detract from their own sense of self-worth. They have such a huge external threat that they must have external help. The attitude is, "Good, come help us. Let's get down to business."

In Nicaragua, unlike in the United States, one doesn't feel like a fool when you put your energies into humanitarian endeavors, into improving people's lives. Absolute dedication and self-sacrifice are abundant here, and it pays, it works. Unfortunately, most Americans don't believe such virtues work.

Q. Why do you think it seems so hard for some internationalists to get integrated here even when they work hard and commit themselves to join the revolution?

I frankly am not sure, entirely. In part, I think it's difficult for Nicaraguans to fully accept someone who maintains citizenship elsewhere. You know, when the going gets tough enough those people can just bail out, whereas Nicas cannot. Something like the northern freedom fighters in the southern civil rights movement. So, for example, there's a stipulation for FSLN party members that they must have Nicaraguan citizenship. That caused problems for some who had either been members or wanted to be. There were a few, not many, internationalists fighting as combatants with the Frente during the insurrection. They were European and Latin. I'm not aware of any U.S. combatants.

It is hard for a non-Nicaraguan to become a total part of the revolution. If a person is content with working on a certain level, a technical level, without advancing into political decision-making, being in the center of things, then one can have some input, and be quite happy for some time. But a person who strives toward total integration will probably be unhappy.

(A woman about 30 appears in the doorway. She wears an FSLN-slogan emblazoned T-shirt and faded blue jeans, her short blond hair pulled tightly at the back of her head, wet with rain.)

Hey, what 'ya doing, Fred?

Sheyla! Good to see you. We were just talking. Hey, what 'ya got in the bag? Something we oughta be eating?

I don't know. Suit yourself.

Explain it to me, please.

I don't know. It's something I bought coming up. It's corn...You never seen it?

Naw. What is it? It's good. It's like a sausage.

It's not a sausage! It's corn dough here and corn dough there, and, like chile inside, and a little bit of coloring.

Pretty good. Not everything you bring is good, but this is.

Almost everything, and almost *everybody* I bring.

I didn't used to think so. I think I'm getting used to it by now. Always rice and beans, rice and beans, and maybe a cold tortilla. And I actually enjoy it. Oh, God!

That's the final stage, Fred. It took you a long time to get into it.

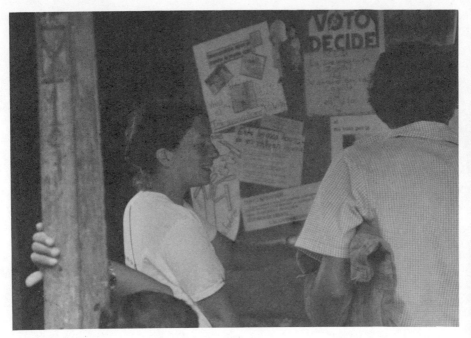

Sheryl Hirshon

photo: Ron Ridenour

Sheryl (Sheyla) Hirshon
This Is My Revolution, Too

Sheryl's parents believed in the American Dream, a hot-selling fantasy in Boston the year of her birth, 1950. Sheryl studied at Antioch College. After acquiring teaching credentials, she founded an alternative school in Portland, Oregon, where she taught basic skills to drug abusers. Now known as "Sheyla," she speaks plainly and sharply.

I became emotionally disgusted with everything in the United States. It was ideological. At college, I couldn't identify with the radical yellers. I just didn't like the fancy shops, fashions, Hostess cupcakes, baseball, driving, card games, the endless manipulations. I do like ice cream, though. I knew the United States was killing people all over the world. I saw no alternative there. I saw no point to working nor to drugs, and there were no political parties worth their salt. I kept asking myself, "What you gonna do girl?" Here I was, well-educated yet having nothing to do with it. So, I took off for Latin America. Lived for a year, 1975-6, on savings, traveling on buses a lot, learning Spanish that way. I was shocked to see Colombia. Such good earth, and yet a wasteland of poverty. I learned the seriousness of being just a little political. In Colombia, Argentina, Central America, being political often meant your life. Even in Costa Rica, the supposed mecca of Latin America, I was thrown out of the country simply because I had a backpack on. The authorities were suspicious of us "types," you know, and I wasn't even one of "them."

I returned to the United States more serious. I ought to do something, I thought. There was nothing I could really do in Latin America, and as a citizen of the problem-maker, I should work within for a change. It took me all of two, maybe three weeks to learn there was nothing I could really do. The United States is a giant plate of jello. You can touch it, but you can't put a mark on it. It springs right back.

People are not real in the U.S. I couldn't believe them. I became very pessimistic, and moped around a lot. Sometimes I thought, "OK Sheryl, take a waitress job, save money and go to India or someplace." Then I'd go into a restaurant and see the forced smiles on the waitresses' faces, and the assholes they had to serve. Oh, God! Not that. After a month of this, I finally got a job teaching at an elementary school. In those days, there were still some government funds for delinquent kids. If you were somewhat educated and a little weird, or had any affinity for social change, then you worked with the "unfit." So, I fell into that. I worked two years and visited Mexico. I also saw some of Cuba and was impressed. I confirmed that the problem was the United States and not me. But what could I do? It is pointless: that was my basic line. It still is. Maybe in 200 years.

Q. Why?

It has a lot to do with the United States' historic role, its geography, its luck in being the capitalistic nation that followed Europe's pioneering, traumatic transition from feudalism to capitalism. Now, the U.S. exports transnationals, multi-national conglomerates. The bulk of the working class it exploits doesn't live in its headquartered country. In fact, U.S. workers are by and large well off, and they know it. Moreover, they are a shrinking class. And they have bought so much divisionary shit, so much obfuscation: white skin privilege, national chauvinism, anti-communism. The population is basically scared and fundamentally materialist. It is not possible to make a revolution if the power structure can promise a better material life. On a gut level, most Americans believe that liberation for people around the world is a material threat to their standard of living.

I just couldn't look on at the evils. I had to participate. There seemed no way but to find another place to work, to live. Cuba seemed to be doing quite well without me. A friend and I took off for Mexico in June of 1979. We thought we might go to Africa. Maybe Mozambique could use us. I hoped it would take a long time to get disillusioned. Then the war for liberation broke out in Nicaragua. We were close and received good information about events. Six weeks after the triumph, we bused down. The air was electric. People were just like us, but they weren't misfits. They were the masses. I jerked my head a lot to check myself. My God! We won something.

The literacy crusade was announced in September 1979. I couldn't merely look on as the Nicaraguan people marshaled to rebuild their shattered country, nor could I return home to a world of hopeless social projects, defeated before they began. Together with volunteers from all over the world, including three from the United States, I joined the one-hundred and eighty thousand Nicaraguan brigadistas who stepped forward to teach their sisters and brothers to read and write.

(Father Fernando Cardenal, director of the literacy crusade, said: "Literacy is fundamental to achieving progress and it is essential to the building of a democratic society where people can participate consciously and critically in national decision-making. You learn to read and write so you can identify the reality in which you live, so that you can become a protagonist of history rather than a spectator."

After the five-month tour of duty in a remote area of Matagalpa province, Sheyla's 25 teenager brigadistas had brought literacy to 123 peasants. She describes the life they led and the beginnings of basic change in the social order in a witty, warmly written book, And Also Teach Them To Read, *published in 1983 by Lawrence Hill & Company, Westport, Connecticut.)*

I robbed the title from Carlos Fonseca. It was also the motif of the literacy crusade. One time during the long war of liberation, Carlos walked up to fellow guerrillas teaching some peasants how to load and clean a weapon, and said to his comrades: "And also teach them to read."

In And Also Teach Them To Read, *Sheila wrote:*

Then it was time to begin the final preparations–the training and the mobilization. The training workshops were impeccably planned two week sessions with agendas posted in advance. They covered everything from methodology to malaria symptoms, from sanitation to statistics. We discussed the goals of the crusade, practiced teaching by role-playing, simulated the debates we hoped the lessons would encourage, developed songs and sociodramas and practiced collective problem-solving. The stress was on creativity. We learned there were other tasks for us, too, in this once in a lifetime mobilization. We were to provide an example of better hygiene habits to people who did not make the connection between this and health. We were to collect folklore traditions and note local flora and fauna. We were also to keep a field diary of all our most significant experiences. This idea had come from the valuable journals kept by some of the guerrillas during the years of struggle.

Diary note from first day, March 24, 1980:

The afternoon grows hotter and sleepier as I wait and watch blankly. Dirt streets with no cars, a wilted market, and a few tired passers-by. It's a county seat in Iowa on a summer afternoon a hundred years ago. It feels like I'm on the wrong set. Night now. There are stars and a meeting by lamplight. Muy Muy doesn't have electricity...We lay our mats out on the bare floor of an empty house, just Estela and me now. There's utter silence in town, and when I blow out this candle it'll be completely dark. Sleep, then. Wait and see.

Diary note, April 1:

There was a moment today, a sight that stopped me dead.... Late afternoon, sun just getting low–and there in back of the dilapidated shack near the gate, the first class beginning. On a bench against the wall, five or six campesinos sit intently, books open on their laps. The tiniest children crawl about a piece of plastic that has been set out for them, while other children, still too young to study, pull impatiently at their mother's skirts. With equal impatience they are brushed away. "Be good now, mother's studying." The brigadista standing before them all with extraordinary naturalness explaining, helping, guiding the work-roughened hands. Dark faces squinting in the lowering sun, dark fingers tracing the letters.

***

It was Orlando, though, who was hurting the most–such a tiny boy, with wide serious eyes. "Rafael's my cousin. Yeah, I knew he was going to leave. He wanted me to go, too, but I said no.... it's our duty as revolutionaries to help the oppressed here. Are you a Catholic? Well, Jesus said to love our brothers, and that means I have to sacrifice myself even if sometimes I want to go home. Have you ever read about Che Guevara, *profe*? He was an internationalist. That's want I want to be. I could lend you the book if you want."

It was almost night when Orlando's bravado broke down, and his smooth delicate face twisted with conflict. "Sometimes I think I just can't take it. Only at night. But I know how important it is and no matter how much it hurts I'm going to try and stay." Che and revolution and God, a dedication he wasn't quite big enough for yet. He'd asked too much of himself. I had to contain the impulse to hug him and tell him to go on home and be a child for another year or two. Instead, I reminded him how much we needed him, how important it was that he stay.

"I know," he said, and as I walked away, I found myself thinking of all the Nicaraguan children who had left their childhoods behind for the revolution, and how many never came back to finish them.

(Eight ex-National Guardsmen crossed the border from Honduras yesterday and murdered the literacy teacher Georgino Andrade—news broadcast, May 19, 1980).

Georgino wasn't a teenager from the city, but a campesino living in one of the villages further north. Coordinator of the local CDS, chief of the militia, and a member of the alphabetization subcommission. This made him a target for the bands of embittered ex-Guardsmen who lived just across the nearby Honduran border.

At first the only thing certain was the survivor's story: "It was around 7:30 at night, when we were reading a book by Che—Georgino and I. All of a sudden, several uniformed men appeared. They grabbed both of us and forced us to leave the house. They asked me if I was a brigadista. I told them no, but they were after Georgino anyway. They took him off. The face they wore as well as the style of talking was of Somoza's guard.

"That same night, we began to look for him. But it wasn't until the next day that we found his body. It had multiple perforations and all his teeth had been broken."

...Georgino Andrade was converted overnight into a symbol, a challenge to the nation to carry through with the literacy crusade whatever the consequences.

For the blood spilled
We'll finish the crusade
A nation of literates
Or die in the crusade

Georgino was the first martyr of the alphabetization; he was not to be the last.

***

What first caught my attention was a look I couldn't quite define. It radiated from every fiber of his slight, dark body—the look of someone with a dream and a decision. It had something to do with a tightness always with him—body erect, military style—and an intensity, almost overintensity of concentration. Little by little I plumbed the depths of his quiet intensity and his dream.

Matías was nineteen and had just finished his first year of high school. He came from a poor family just outside Managua. His mother and migrant father were now both dead, leaving two other sons and a daughter. The scars on Matías's face were from a childhood bout with chicken pox. "In these countries," he told me with an ironic smile, "poor people's children get sick. It's rare to find one who doesn't have scars of some kind."

We'd walk all over the hills when I came to visit, talking about everything in the world. He believed in the revolution, in the rights of the workers and peasants to the fruits they created, in short, in Marxism-Leninism. He said so proudly, right out loud.

Q. What did you do after the crusade?

55

When the crusade was over, I didn't know what I was going to do. About that time they were changing all the immigration rules. There was this whole business about papers, and I got nervous about any new job possibilities. It was all so undefined. First they said I could, then I couldn't. I didn't know the steps. I mean, nobody did. The first year you could do anything you wanted. The second year, they began to organize, and of course that's the worst phase.

I didn't want to go back to the United States. I left wanting to leave, and I was so excited when I found out I was right. I felt like somebody took a pack of rocks off my back. I didn't miss anything. And to this day, I must say, I really don't. I don't know what's wrong with me. I mean, you're supposed to feel homesick. You're supposed to go to bed and think, "Gee, I wish I had a Betty Crocker Chocolate cake, but I don't wish it that much. I went back to the States once. I was there 18 days. It was all right. I talked to my friends and went to the stores. It's the same place. I was reconfirmed. I returned and spoke with the education minister and the director.

Q. In Managua?

No, here, the region of Matagalpa. We're far from Managua. I must confess I don't know anything about the Capitol nor the commandantes, and actually don't care to. I mean, they're nice people and I like them, I just don't think they are the center of the revolution.

All my life has been in Matagalpa. I don't even like Managua. Anyway, I got a job teaching English in a high school. I learned a bit of Miskito as I was going to teach English to some Indians who had been resettled in our department. But teaching in secondary school is much like it is in the States. It hasn't changed a lot. It means having 500 students and teaching 12 classes to people who are tired. They are more adult in attitudes, but English is an obligatory subject, and few are really interested in learning it. They just want that passing grade. What I really wanted to do was adult education. After agonizing over it for months, I got the transfer after the school term. So, I've been on staff as a technical assistant for three years, one at Muy Muy and two working out of La Delia. I love it.

Q. Why don't you like Managua?

It's too hot, too confusing. I never found my way around. It's like going to New York City, a nice place to visit for a day. It's another country in another century. People's complaints, problems are very different. When you first come here and walk into people's houses you are shocked. They have nothing–a homemade stool, bench, table, three plates, a corn milling machine, some clothes and a little box somewhere–but they'll give you anything. If they have a bed, they'll let you sleep in it. Whatever food they have, is yours. And they'll talk with you about how much better their lives are. But in Managua, where all foreigners come, especially journalists, you hear nothing but complaints about how little they have. Even when you are in a market place surrounded by more things than you'll see in a month in the country, people say, *no hay nada* (there is nothing). You just go, "Oh, Christ!"

Q. What is your day like?

My work day begins about 5:30, with sunup usually. I turn on *Puno en Alto* (fist in the air), the official radio program of our adult education program. It broadcasts twice a day over all stations and gives the latest dope from Managua about what we're supposed to be doing, and letters are read, like letters from home. The program generally shares CEP (Collectives of Popular Sandinista Education) progress and difficulties. Then I bathe, eat, and start off to work.

Mine is a varied job: checking on the quality of teaching in the classrooms, orienting promoters (who monitor problems of students and teachers), consolidating student statistics and lessons, giving workshops to coordinators and promoters. After learning the fundamentals, adults can study up to six levels, or grades. Each year we've added a new level, and teach coordinators to advance students. We teach only language and math, but MED (Ministry of Education) plans more subjects as well as more levels, up to nine.

We are slowly developing a dual educational system where kids go to primary school in the mornings and adults go to school in the late afternoon or evening, depending on circumstances. In most rural communities, both systems operate side by side out of the same building. The actual problem is that the countryside is so vast and with such a scattered population that it is still difficult to have schools for all the children.

(In the first three years of the revolution, Nicaragua doubled the number of schools from 2,681 to 5,377, with 160,000 new desks for one million total students, also double 1979 figures. The amount of funds allocated for education rose from two percent of the GDP to five percent. By 1984, there were 20,000 CEPs teaching 165,000 adult students, and involving 16,000 volunteer promoters and coordinators. In Sheyla's zone, there were 129 coordinators, down from 170 the year before, and 32 promoters. There were six technical assistants to oversee the work and lessons for 12,000 people of school age. By early 1984, the contra "freedom fighters" had murdered 102 popular education teachers, promoters and coordinators, and burned down or forced the closure of scores of schools, and virtually halting new school construction.)

In my zone, every fold in every mountain has a little core of houses. At the time of the revolution, there were three public schools, now there are 80. With regional decentralization, La Dalia has become an educational coordinating center. This truck stop junction now has its first telephone office and lines, a medical clinic with two doctors, and a militia unit. Our department has the nation's highest concentration of rural workers and campesinos in the most scattered, mountainous terrain. It is also the most backward department with 33 percent illiteracy, down only seven percent from the end of the literacy crusade. The overall national illiteracy figure is 13 percent. We work on it all the time, organizing communities that haven't yet been involved.

To begin in a new community, we ask everybody to assemble and we explain the adult education program. We find people who can read and write, the key people who can help. If there is a union, it will sometimes assist us. It is usually just chance finding people to help out. Sometimes it is someone you never would have expected. A shy little campesina turns out to be dynamite as a teacher or organizer. Sometimes you walk into a house and hear someone speaking who sounds great, right down the line, and they are just good for nothing. Another sounds wonderful before you learn that he got drunk last year and sold the lamp.

Q. Sold the lamp?

Yeah, MED loans the popular educators lamps for studying at night. The worst thing you can do is get drunk and sell the lamp.

I attend to seven promoters scattered over an area that takes two days to cover, if you walk straight. Often I have to walk four, five or more hours to observe how a class is going. Bicycles are useless on these roads and non-roads. And we don't have a horse. In my last zone, I often was loaned a horse. Frankly I hate riding. A horse never pays any attention to me. I'd rather go on foot because I just end up having a battle of wills with an animal who has the last word. When it is real muddy and I have to go up hills, and there is a horse, I'll lower my pride and ride the animal, frustrated. But where I am now, we don't have any access to horses. Once someone here loaned me a mule. It ran off. I got pissed, so I don't borrow it anymore.

When you do find a great promoter it is tremendous. They are amazing people. They do a voluntary job–MED now pays a stipend of 500 cordobas a month for promoters and 200 for coordinators–after their hard work day. Often, they have a natural intelligence that leaves you speechless. Almost none of them have any education beyond the rudiments learned through the literacy crusade. The promoter usually finds the coordinators, who teach two hours a day. Then there are some promoters you have to watch and coax, who don't do much. Sometimes I have to find replacements, like when somebody has a jealous husband who doesn't want his wife out of the house. The student is still the weakest link. They require a lot of motivation, a lot of reassurance. Adult students are very delicate, they'll desert classes at any moment for any reason: personal problems, work, politics, the contra war of course. Usually they are learning because they are interested, but they have no history of education. They see little use in following the course from beginning to end, in getting a diploma. It's just not in their frame of reference. For them, it is fine if this year they learn to read, next year learn to add, but they don't get to the part about subtracting.

Eighty percent of our teachers don't know how to teach well. You can't blame them. They've never been properly educated, or at all. The teaching method is difficult. To do it right, you have to have a lot of self-confidence to begin with. You have to have a certain subtlety to direct a conversation with a student, and encourage them to express themselves. Then you have the problem of having ten students on different levels, or if on the same level they don't all show up, and some get behind. We also don't get teachers very long for training, maybe one or two weekend days a month for workshops, and four days at the beginning of the semester. So our most important task is to attend the classes, observing how they are doing and correct as we go along. We spend one or two hours, or half the night explaining what is going right and wrong, trying to encourage. Sometimes students desert because the teacher may not be terribly competent. The students go on and on and don't feel like they are learning anything. And those who are alphabetizing now are mostly hard rock cases, after five years of revolution and educational programs everywhere. Many have made the attempt before and just have memory problems, or they lose their materials. Every adult student gets free note-pads, pencils once a month, and a book. But there are not enough so we can readily replace those destroyed or lost.

Q. You must get frustrated.

Nothing ever works right in this program. Frustrations are accepted as part of daily living. We *do* get results, regardless of my expressed cynicism, so ulcers are avoided. We've been giving workshops to promoters and coordinators. Last week I just finished the series underway for 18 months. It takes a lot of time. People have to come from a large area. Sleeping and eating arrangements must be made, and there is no ready transportation. There are always competing activities, too. Well, anyway, we've finished. The numbers were small, but just look at these people. I don't know, it is just astounding. The love they have for learning, the effort they put into getting ahead. They are mostly in their mid-20s, people who never had a chance to get an education, and never would have without the revolution. Now, they are motivated, excited, and receiving the equivalent of a fifth grade diploma. They'll teach, and some will go on to have my job.

Q. Critics say the program indoctrinates students in communism.

There is a certain amount of politics in the program, I can't deny that. But what we do is teach students to be critical, to evaluate. They look at a picture in the lesson book and explain what they think it is. If it involves the revolution or the FSLN, the student is certainly able to disagree. The important thing is to develop a critical attitude. Most peasants haven't had such opportunities and don't analyze. Analyzing is a stumbling block to most; it doesn't come easily.

Q. Why does the revolution put so much effort into education?

The revolution needs people to think. It is trying to build popular power. In my work, one can get an idylic view of the revolution. However, there are many people who are still greedy, mendacious, and also poor. You also see so many who are honest and generous and sincere and never had a chance to do anything. These are the people the revolution needs. Living in the countryside, you actually come to your own conclusion that this *is* a popular revolution. It's not what's happening in Managua that counts, it's the participation of the people that is going to make or break the revolution. It's easy to see in the mountains that if you have an apathetic, helpless population feeling it can't make changes, then you just kill the revolution. It will fail no matter who your comandantes are. I hope that the opposite is also true–that if you have a population that not only is intelligent but also understands what their rights are, what a revolution means–that the revolution can't fail. We tell people that they must watch out, that in 20 years the revolution might not be here if they are not active in it. The people are the guardians. That's why the State and the FSLN are educating people. That is how you make a revolution.

Q. Is that what motivates you?

Yeah. I think it's a privilege to work in the revolution. I feel extremely lucky. I meet people from abroad who have felt the same hopelessness I've felt in the States. Most of my friends in the U.S. write me saying they envy me. In spite of the fact that my life has certainly become more difficult materially–I'm getting to sound like a Nica, bitching and moaning that I can't get this and that–but it is very secondary. I feel fantastic using what talents I have to move something along that is very important. I get the feeling I'm helping push a big, big train along. It's a feeling you never get if you live in the United States. The best thing you can do is throw rocks at a big, big train that is going in a direction you wish it weren't going. Your rocks are never going to stop the train anyway. But here, the train is going in the right direction, and I'm helping it with so many wonderful people. Yeah, I'm lucky.

Q. Are the contras a problem in your work?

Yes. It cannot be denied. A bit north of us, for example, in San Rafael del Norte, there were 1,000 adult students last year. Sixty-three are graduating this year, when we should have had twice that many. That's sad. It's enough that people have to risk their lives just to go to work in the fields. Few want to risk their lives to study, although promoters and coordinators are usually willing to. So, yes, the contras have their little victories.

Just last week, contras came through our zone. They burned three houses and the coffee processing plant on a UPE (State farm). It was a beautiful State farm, one of the nicest and best organized. The people were not armed. You can't arm everybody in Nicaragua, nor can you give, like, three weapons to a community because they can't stave off a serious attack, and more people get killed. So tactics have been changed to where some places are thoroughly armed in self-defense, or are protected by an army unit, while others go unarmed. They just hope the contras won't kill them. Well, this band seemed more exploratory than on the kill, and they stayed three days, unfortunately. According to the people—whom I know well—the contras played cards and baseball, slept in the family houses and ate their food. They were up high and could see any oncoming attack. Our army was on another mountain range, engaged in a battle with another band. But still nobody knows why it took three full days before any rescue units came, maybe because the contra had all those civilians. And that's the key political problem, the insecurity of not knowing. In another community attacked nearby, eight women were raped repeatedly. But not here. The contra got everyone together and told them not to work for the State, not to organize or participate in any social, educational or health projects. Finally, the contra retreated. The people were terrorized and abandoned the UPE en masse. They were resettled temporarily, and are still unsure what they are going to do. The coffee is still there to be picked, but the people want guarantees of protection. Many of the coordinators are also too frightened to give classes, and those who are determined to do so have no one attending them. The cheap political trick of the contra is to tell people that they must be careful because they are leaving informers. So, many are afraid to participate in anything. We've had experiences where this trauma takes about three months to work itself out. Here, in this model community, my work fell apart, at least for the time being. Now, we must convince our students to take the final exam and be tallied. Part of our job is bureaucratic, turning in statistics so the international organizations that support us see results.

Q. Are you afraid to be in the countryside so close to war?

I don't have any particular fear for myself. I'm not trying to be noble or anything, but nothing bad ever happens to me. I'm somewhat scared in the city because that's what I've been conditioned to fear. The one exception in the countryside is rivers. I wasn't afraid of them until they dumped me over a few times. Several brigadistas were drowned during the literacy campaign because city folks don't know how powerful a rain-filled river is. The countryside is so peaceful, so beautiful. I've been where the contra have passed through and it just seems impossible. You'd think you'd see green smoke or rumblings of thunder if contras were about.

If they happened to capture me, I imagine they'd beat me up and try to terrorize me, but wouldn't kill me. Yet many are uncontrollable, twisted. It depends on the moment, on who captures you. There are random killings and then there are people who probably feel thay are doing an "honest" job as a mercenary for pay. I may be too calm about it–you can always have bad luck. I mean, they did come through nearby to an unorganized private farm and cut the throats of eight campesinos who were doing nothing.

I do fear for my colleagues. I have friends who have been brutally killed. There have been three, four...Christ, *seven* of my fellow technical assistants killed. There are only about a hundred of us. One just died in Río Blanco last week, not far from my zone. There's another wounded right now. It gets creepy. You just don't know, it's like, who's next. It affects your emotional life. For months now we have been living in a permanent state of war. Sometimes I get terribly angry. When I let myself think about it, I'm outraged. It gets even worse when I read something like the Senate approves more money to the contras. You just can't believe it. It's not so upsetting to read about Reagan. He's the villain, so he acts like one and you say, well he does what villains do. But then you read the U.S. press, hear what Congress and the Establishment institutions do, how people vote. It's the worst of what I know, but still wish weren't true. I say a lot of cynical things, especially about the States, but they are true. Here you are working so hard for things that are so simple. All of a sudden these beasts come to topple over what we've been sweating to build up. You just get outraged.

People in the United States don't want to look beyond what is convenient to see. They are *babosa* (Literally *babosa* implies a slug, but it also implies an idiot.) I suppose in some way, they suspect that their daily comforts are dependent upon the misery of others. I must say, it took me by surprise that people, the evil people, are really as evil as they told you they were. But here we are.

Q. If the contras, or the Yankees, attack, will you fight?

Sure. I've been close, heard shots, but not had a chance to shoot. I'm prepared to defend myself...but I don't know if I'm *prepared*.

You know, Nicaraguans ask me the same thing: will you fight your own people. I remind them they fought their own people, the Somocistas.

Q. Are you thinking about naturalization?

I've thought about it. I must say I was a bit sad during the elections. It was the only time I felt marginalized. But I didn't feel too bad since I knew the FSLN was going to win, and had plenty of propagandizers. If it had looked close, I would have felt real bad not being able to participate. I think I'm going to stay in Nicaragua, but giving up my passport is a worry. It doesn't worry me so much that I might not be able to participate in another country. I'd be identified with a Nicaragua passport, and couldn't go to so many places. And I wouldn't have anymore effectiveness with a change in citizenship. I'd have more legal participation, but I'd also be an embarrassment. You can't get around not having Nica ancestry. It bothers me a bit that I can't go all the way in political life, but not often, only when I might not strongly agree with something. I mean, the worst you get is incompetence on the base level. Occasionally, you get someone who is a petty tyrant in the making, but they don't last long. I've seen things that made me go *eeeiii*, you blew it, but never saw anything that was a disaster that wasn't later repaired. If you see an illegality, as I have from time to time, you report it, wheels turn, and it gets rectified. There have been abuses, serious ones: like drafting kids who weren't old enough, by law. Draft boards members are given a quota, see, and well, many still do not respect the law, and just don't report. Draft day comes and those responsible only meet half their quota. This happened on the day of the last July 19th anniversary in Matagalpa. Draft board staff went around picking up kids and sent them off. It had terrible repercussions. Yet here is an example where what the revolution is trying to do has good implications. The same government that trains the people to be critical, makes a misstep, and the people protest. All the labor organizations, especially the Sandinista ones, and representatives of all the community organizations protested loud and clear. People went to the Frente personally. Those who could prove they were underage were returned home. Some probably are still in the military. Memos were circulated warning against any repeats. The people were vindicated, but many don't know it and remain distrustful.

Q. How do you describe yourself politically?

I guess I've become a Sandinista, of sorts, ha. I think Freud had the best line on that. He said, "Well, I'd consider myself a

Marxist but the serious Marxists wouldn't have me." I haven't studied Marxism. I guess I'm a bit lazy about it. I'm tired at the end of the day's work, and if I read at all, I'd rather read a novel.

Q. Why do some internationalists, Marxists especially, have so hard a time integrating in revolutionary Nicaragua?

I have the impression that may be why you don't find the dedicated foreign Marxists here, because people who come thinking that want to influence the political process are the first ones to get frustrated. But people who love the country and the political process, and aren't particularly upset when they discover their political participation is limited, that doesn't bother them. It's something they'd already encountered in their own country.

Q. So you have no dilemma working for the revolution yet having no formal political connection?

It concerns me a bit, but the thing is I like what I'm doing so much, in part, because there are so few cadres and, bizarre as it may sound, I get nearer the political process. I like what is going on. The moment I don't I'm gonna become a very unhappy person. If there is something I don't like at work and it's in an area outside my authority, then I can talk with someone in the process and try to get them to see my point so they'll talk about it. But the day I go here, and they go there–if that day ever comes–I may as well leave because there is nothing I can do. I accept that. You see, I'm real pleased to be doing something that is useful within a process that seems to me to be so perfectly reasonable. I've seen so much progress, especially in the countryside. Besides, I never had very high expectations of what was going to happen to me, so I'm elated.

Q. Do you meet any resistance or harassment for being who you are?

No. People are extremely accepting. I'm identified in the good slot as a teacher, *profe* they call me. In the countryside, people get so used to me, nobody reacts to me as a foreigner. I get no harassment for that or for being white, but occasionally for being a woman, though actually less than if I were a Nicaraguan woman. With me there is a certain hands-off attitude. People do find it strange, even astounding, that I walk around the countryside by myself. Nicaraguan women will always be accompanied. I just hate bothering people, and most of all, I like to walk alone.

(Sheyla gleefully climbs into my rented vehicle early Sunday morning, looking forward to picking up hitchhikers she'll probably know as we drive the 50 kilometers northeast to La Dalia. The road outside Matagalpa soon turns to dirt and rock, more holes than surface. We travel at 10 to 20 kilometers an hour, stopping periodically to pick up one or two persons, even a family complete with chickens. Climbing higher into tall trees, we observe a group of fluffy clouds hanging about mountain peaks as far as the eye can see. Suddenly, we come to a plateau dotted with a score of wooden huts: La Dalia, a two-dirt-road town. At the edge of town, the education office stands next to Comedor Liliam, *the one-room local eating place. A horse stands in front, a handful of chickens rush past, a black pig grunts by, flies and bees buzz around. On the porch, a sign proclaiming "Your Vote Decides" is fixed over a big chalk board filled with the year's literacy figures. On another chart, the figure 1,837 indicates the number of adult students enrolled in grades one through five. Of the 1,085 remaining, Sheyla estimates half will pass the final exams.*

Sheyla's rented room of irregular plywood and concrete floor is just a few paces behind the office porch. Inside hangs a bare electric line connected crudely to a bare 40-watt light bulb, a recent advance over the lantern she used exclusively for years. On the only table in the room sits a portable radio. Sheyla makes her coffee on a kerosene burner. Four or five changes of clothes hang on a line stretched across the six-foot wide windowless room. A bucket of water sits in the middle. Resting on the wall by the folded cot stands Sheyla's loaded automatic rifle.

We walk through the town, stopping to chat with a man selling a campesino a newspaper. She invites the education promoter to use his home for a class next semester. He says he's been sick, that's why he dropped his promoting tasks. She nods understandingly, and he agrees to use his house. At the school, the 20-year-old teacher is visibly pregnant. Her third level class of 18 teenagers, middle-aged men, and handful of women with small children hanging about, is bent over notebooks writing answers to the two questions on the blackboard: What are the boundaries of Nicaragua? Name the countries of Central America and describe the actual state of affairs in one. After conversing with the teacher, Sheyla and I continue our walk.)

The one bad moment in the morning is the precarious walk through mud to the latrine. If I'm lucky, I can pee outside in the dark. To wash, I must get water from the well, but it dries up in the summer. You have to go to the river then.

When organizing, I often truck my portable cot around like a vagrant from community to community. I eat at campesinos' homes, beans and rice and tortillas mostly. I eat all the food and drink all the water, and I've never been sick. It's very strange. Someday I'm going to die of it, ha. Neither I nor the Nicaraguans understand it. They joke with me about being in the CIA: "How come she never gets sick?" Everybody I know gets sick. I've never taken a pill or seen a doctor. Then there are days on end when I stay in town. Usually I find somebody to cook for me because it's a lot of work to cook for yourself if you work full-time. You have to find things and build a fire, wash pots. Everything takes a lot more time than in the States. There are no machines or robots. Right now the staff is eating at Café Liliam. It's like a boarding house. I used to sleep in the office, but it was inconvenient. Now, I rent this room for one hundred cordobas a month, and split the Matagalpa rent of 400 ($15). Our school year is nearly over now. I want to be sent to pick coffee after final exams. We are supposed to maintain an office staff during the harvest, but we can never get students in any numbers on a regular basis. Most of the technical assistants will be studying, and I don't want to be the fall guy in the office. It's like being in the eye of a hurricane with nothing to do. I like picking coffee. It's hard work, fun, and productive.

Q. What do you do for your social life?

Within limits, the people I work with are like brothers and sisters. We kind of know each other inside and out. We insult each other, beat one another up. As far as casual conversation with people, I have as many here as I ever did in the States. Sometimes I find I don't talk about my life before Nicaragua. Often we talk superficially, or about ideas and politics. People here don't have the custom of speaking very personally. They are not into analyzing themselves. But sometimes I do get lonely. I have dated Nica men. I've had my disasters. I still have hope.

Q. What are your future plans?

Just what I am doing. I may be transferred, but I'll keep on with what I'm doing here or in another war zone. I believe in my work. This is my revolution, too.

Doug Murray   *photo: Ron Ridenour*

Doug Murray

Pesticides, the Smell of Nicaragua

(Leopoldina: "I worked for a while at Babilonia, the hacienda out by the road. But it was terrible, you can't imagine how bad, cooking for all those mozos [hired hands] from four in the morning to nine at night sometimes. Then we had to sleep in a room full of pesticide sacks that turned out to be poisonous. I didn't know what was happening, but the kids kept getting sicker and sicker until finally I got desperate enough to take them to Matagalpa where they told me that they'd been poisoned. They'd just escaped dying on me." —From And Also Teach Them To Read.*)*

Doug Murray grew up in California's wine rich Napa Valley countryside, which afforded him the early experience of harvesting fruit crops and learning about work hazards such as pesticides. After a stint as a reporter for the local newspaper, he moved to San Francisco and went to work for the State. He soon returned to college as a teacher and later acquired a doctorate in sociology. He took a job with OSHA (Occupational Safety and Health Administration), testing the effects of pesticide poisoning on workers. Murray arrived in Nicaragua in 1983 to see first hand the new Nicaragua and to continue a relationship with a woman working with the revolution. After interviews at the Ministry of Labor (MITRAB), he was put on as Technical Advisor on Pesticide Hazards, one of two U.S. citizens on the Ministry's several hundred-member staff.

Q. What kind of commitment does the Sandinista government have toward protecting people from pesticide poisoning?

73

Central America is one of the worst places in the world for pesticide problems. Nicaragua's revolutionary government is the first in the region to tackle the problem head-on. It has created a coordinating commission, the National Pesticide Commission, which includes the ministries of labor, agriculture, health, natural resources, along with the rural workers union, ATC (Farm Workers Association). The Commission began investigating what could be done but lacked any skilled persons with a background in pesticide safety. Although MITRAB was not really open to hiring North Americans, I came along with the right skills at the right moment.

Unlike most countries where agencies battle each other, the NPC is a comprehensive program of inter-agency cooperation, designed to eliminate in-fighting and streamline work. It also works with the growers' association and pesticides companies. Aside from training inspectors, I started off by making recommendations to the commission, helping to revise Nicaragua's pre-1979 health and safety standards. Among my recommendations is a provision that storage of pesticides should be under lock and key in specially color-coded containers. People in the Third World don't waste anything and store things in whatever is available. Paraquat (the black liquid defoliant used by the DEA against marijuana plants) is often stored in coke bottles. Someone comes along and drinks it. Paraquat is a very deadly defoliant and if ingested almost always results in a slow, agonizing death. We want to stop that. Another key area is in mixing pesticides safely. The tradition is to buy pesticides in barrels of concentrate, and then mix it with water, often while loading it on a plane to spray fields. I recommend a closed mixing system. The concentrate can be siphoned out of the barrel by a diesel-powered pump that can also siphon water from a well or holding tank, and then pump both into the plane without ever having the liquid come in contact with air. The pump has a valve so the water flow can be reversed to wash out the tubes without running the risk of someone being exposed to these chemicals. That is where you get fatalities. Some of these chemicals are incredibly toxic, and kill within hours just from getting on your skin.

Q. How can this poor nation undergoing both an economic boycott and a costly war acquire sufficient machines for this?

One of the things I'm doing here is designing projects and writing proposals for solidarity aid. Right now, I'm negotiating with international firms to set up a facility that would build these closed systems in Nicaragua. We have just about tied up the money. Building the equipment is mostly a soldering, machine tooling job. It will spin off other jobs too, while reducing significantly the illnesses and deaths so extensive in cotton production. I conducted an inspection at an agricultural airfield in Chinandega, for example, where 31 workers out of the crew of 123 sought medical treatment for pesticide poisoning in one month alone. In the United States that would be an unbelievable figure. What happens in this process is that chemicals are spilled on the ground, and the air gets filled with the poison. The entire work area can be easily contaminated. Office workers walking to work get saturated with it, or air conditioning apparatuses suck fumes into offices. A laundry woman gets covered with it from the clothes she must wash. Mechanics working on the planes get contaminated from the buckets of pesticides being slopped into the plane. We hope we can produce and install these closed systems in all work areas where mixing and loading occurs, but the ever-escalating drain on our resources will postpone our project, I'm afraid, until after the war is won.

I'm involved in another project sampling the blood of cotton pickers, pesticide applicators, and airfield workers. We've done 1200 so far in the Chinandega-Leon area, collecting data so we can see what the closed systems accomplish next year.While conducting an educational campaign, instructing workers about pesticide hazards, we treat those we find poisoned. A big problem is just securing a vehicle so we can speed up our inspections. Last year, the Ministry had two vehicles for all its 40 inspectors in health and safety. Right now, we don't have one that is functioning for us. Things change every day. Some of the inspectors go to war against the contras, others are used in harvests. The problem is we never get to complete the training because of the war. I lose more inspector trainees that way, and there is always the nagging fear one will die. One guy I trained, and came to feel real close to, came back last week. I was glad to see him, but he was just here to clear out his desk before being sent back to the front on a more permanent basis. You see, the army gets the best men, the best trained, the more motivated and committed. They are needed to make the reliable split-second decisions that save lives and win battles. Just about all those I get close to, and who learn fast, go to the front. That is the hard part of this job.

Q. Do you have problems communicating when training?

My Spanish is basically street Spanish. It's OK, but I make a lot of mistakes, and people at work crack up sometimes. I've been the subject of a lot of jokes. That is something cultural here. Things that stateside might be thought of as cruel or unkind—leading you on because you don't understand what is going on, and then everybody around you is just laughing themselves silly—really isn't something malicious here. It is actually a sign of acceptance. It took me a long time to understand. I thought people were making fun of me, but they were really accepting me by having a good laugh at my expense.

Our training process is mostly interaction on field trips, looking at problems and potential problems, discussing solutions. I also use slides and give talks on what chemicals do and can do, and about what we can do to avoid or solve problems. About 10 of the Ministry's health and safety personnel are getting training in pesticides.

Q. Regardless of Nicaragua's efforts to control pesticide hazards, pests will continue to plague agriculture and workers' health, will they not?

In Louisiana, there is a statue to the boll weevil (the beetle which damages cotton balls). It reads: The Boll Weevil Won. That is what is happening around the world, the boll weevil wins.

Finding methods in nature to combat the damage done by pests is not profitable for petro-chemical conglomerates, so little is done. That is no longer the case in Nicaragua. The will to find natural ways of combating harmful pests is there, yet the economy and technology is still dependent on hundreds of years of foreign control. As I wrote in a paper about pesticides and the Nicaragua revolution (published by *Policy Studies Review*, November 1984), the pesticide problems of Nicaragua were a classic example of the legacy of the Somoza era and the conditions of underdevelopment generally, inherited by the Sandinistas upon their victory. In the 1950s, cotton became the major export crop in Nicaragua, occupying 40 percent of cultivated land by the mid-1960s. Such concentration of cotton brought with It the boll weevil. Cotton producers bought more and more pesticides from U.S. salesmen, creating a vicious cycle of increased dependency on pesticides as pests developed resistance and new pests emerged when their natural enemies were killed off by the chemical poisons. Malaria-carrying mosquitos became immune to chemical pesticides, causing ever larger outbreaks of the disease. By the mid-60s, Central America accounted for 40 percent of the total U.S. export of pesticides to the hemisphere, and pesticides constituted 31 percent of the region's investments in cotton production. Yet growers still lost one-fifth of their crop to pests. Deaths to workers became daily fare with the introduction of DDT and methyl parathion, a commercial product developed out of nerve gas chemical warfare research. Nicaragua had a *reported* 3,000 annual poisonings during the decade 1962-72, or 176 cases per 1,000 population, eight times that of the United States. In 1969, 383 deaths caused by pesticides were *reported*. Statistics were badly kept and clinics were far and few between. In many cases, the large landowners had their own medical clinics and the staff often hindered the few public health officials from detecting the seriousness of human insecticide poisonings.

Some pesticides cause cancer. The pesticide class known as organochlorines are the most damaging, with DDT and toxaphene among the worst examples. Nicaragua led the world in DDT use in the 1970s, even after it was banned in the U.S. Nicaraguan workers tested were found to contain 16 times the world average of DDT in their fatty tissues, and human breast milk was found to have 45 times the World Health Organization's established maximum tolerance level for DDT.

Upon the triumph, the Sandinistas found themselves confronted with a monumental task as they began to pursue their commitment to transform Nicaraguan society. The government set out to reduce, over the long term, the use of expensive and highly toxic pesticides and, for the present, sought to reduce human poisonings and environmental contaminations caused by excessive and careless pesticide applications. The reduction of Nicaragua's pesticides depends mainly on developing alternative means of pest control, or Integrated Pest Management (IPM). This philosophy makes maximum use of naturally occurring insect controls, using biological, environmental, cultural and legal methods in a complementary manner. Under Somoza, the Food and Agricultural Organization of the United Nations (FAO) began IPM experiments, but the program faltered for lack of government support. The new government reintroduced IPM experiments, and by 1982 MIDINRA (Ministry of Agriculture) was using such methods in one-sixth of the cotton acreage. The main program was "trap cropping," in which four rows of cotton plants per several acres are left after the harvest instead of plowing them under. These plants become the trap for the boll weevil. Before the main crop is planted the following year, another trap is planted next to the existing one in order to continue the concentration of the pest population. By treating the traps with pesticides, the pest problem can be kept down, reducing pesticide treatments on the main crop. The initial experiment resulted in a $2.14 million savings in pesticides costs. In 1983, the program area was tripled and in 1984, trap cropping was made mandatory for all cotton producers. While this method helps, it is limited in usefulness. You are still using pesticides, and the pests still develop resistance within the trap crop, too. Trap cropping is also labor intensive instead of technology intensive. Workers have to attend the crop every day to see what the pest population is doing. If the fields aren't watched closely enough, an outbreak of pests occurs. Bacteria and parasites are also being introduced to control pests now. In fact, the entire Leon area has just had a bacteria introduced to control pests. That is a major advance. Some naturally occurring diseases destroy harmful insects without harming beneficial organisms, including humans.

Despite the efforts so far, which include a newly created university graduate program in IPM, the majority of pest control methods remain chemically dependent. To cope with this dependence, the government controls pesticide imports, and has banned the worst. Only one pesticide is locally produced, toxaphene, and the plant is being considered for conversion in order to produce safer products.

Pesticide safety is a major focus of the 4,000 safety classes MITRAB has thus far conducted, and the Ministry of Health has made pesticide illness one of its major priorities. Still, many obstacles exist to the government's ambition to eliminate pesticide poisonings. Naturally, there is a limit of funds, a scarcity of material resources and trained personnel, as well as social habits formed during hundreds of years of unrestrained exploitation of human, animal and plant life. Bad habits are not broken quickly. But the major obstacle is the combined political-economic-military aggression from the United States. The possibility that new policies might briefly disrupt foreign exchange earnings is a powerful brake against implementing any alternative course of action. In addition, as much as 40 percent of the national budget is used for defense-related spending. The constant need for mobilizations of useful workers, including government inspectors, to defend communities and harvests have eaten into social programs' progress. By the end of 1983, 18 of the 40 MITRAB health and safety inspectors had been mobilized to fight the contra or to harvest coffee with arms on hand. Ten MIDINRA technicians have been murdered in ambushes while on inspection. And when the port of Corinto was attacked by boats launched from a CIA supply ship (October 10, 1983), part of the supply of pesticides used to control the boll weevil was destroyed, leaving many cotton fields with no means to combat the pest. Supply ships were disrupted for months afterward, causing further serious shortages of pesticides. The government had to use whatever materials were available. Undesirable, dangerous pesticides stored away were reintroduced for that harvest, a significant setback in Nicaragua's efforts to improve the environment and health of her people. Yet I have hope for vast improvement, if only the war would end.

Q. How do you assess the Ministry's effectiveness in conducting safety programs and promoting safe conditions for workers?

That has been a hard learning process for me. I come from the most developed nation in the world with huge resources and an arrogant chip on its shoulder. It affects us all. I got frustrated at first with what was bureaucratic inefficiency. Things went too slowly and I thought a lot of opportunities were missed. The longer I stay the more I understand the complexities of life here, particularly the hardship of living in war. It has been humbling. I now realize how impressive any little accomplishment is. I used to get upset when people wouldn't show for meetings, or inspections would get cancelled, or a penalty rendered an employer was so minimal, no change would be attractive to him. But now I've learned: vehicles break down and there are no replacement parts; something more important than pesticides comes up, and the telephones don't work so they can't call me; employers have to be educated too, and imposing a more severe penalty at a time when the government wants to encourage employees, especially private enterprise, to participate and produce, is at times an unwarranted deterrent.

Not long ago, we were to fly into Potosi, on the Gulf of Fonseca, for two days of inspections. Just as we were about to leave, Potosi got bombed, so we didn't go there for a couple months. I wanted to go earlier, but when I got there I saw that production had ground to a halt. A lot of things just didn't happen for months after the attack that destroyed some of the equipment, and frightened workers away from the fields. It just wasn't appropriate for me to be there, nor was there much to inspect for some time. Nicaraguans understand the priorities better than I do, and I have to trust that they do. That is something very, very hard for a United States citizen to accept. But I am learning patience. I do all my novel reading waiting for appointments.

Q. Apart from the war, isn't it also true that Nicaraguans routinely do not explain their thought processes?

Right. You have to figure it out yourself. Over time you have enough experience so you can see things clearly. Explanations aren't a priority. In other words, making it clear to your North American pesticide consultant, sitting down and explaining day after day why something isn't happening, well, there just isn't time.

Q. Yes, that makes sense. But isn't it also true that ordinary Nicaraguans don't give or get explanations? Walking around in the dark is common here. If the revolution is trying to build workers' power—democracy—then workers have to have sufficient information and explanations in order to form opinions and participate in decision-making.

Yes, people do run around in the dark often. I'd explain that as more of a legacy of the past method of rule. They overthrew

Somoza, but they didn't change a hell of a lot else immediately. Many of those in decision-making positions are the same people who were functioning in Somoza's time. Some of the places I inspect are supervised by people who were supervisors before the triumph. It is going to take a long time to change habits. The Sandinista revolution has initiated changes, but it takes years to become institutionalized. That is one purpose of the elections, for instance, to institutionalize new programs and changes of all sorts.

Q. Can workers be effective in their demands without the right to strike?

That's a tough question. I'm not crazy about the fact that they don't have the right to strike. But you have to realize that is an emergency measure imposed by the government because the nation is at war. A war is being fought for the very survival of the national sovereignty (During World War II, the United States outlawed strikes, too).

Workers do have other rights, and they use them. They use them to speak out in the *Cara al Pueblo* (face-to-face meetings with the top leadership). Our Ministry, like others, receives complaints from workers all the time about safety problems and violations of wage laws and agreements. The Ministry has been lambasted by *Barricada* because inspectors or negotiators have met with employers and then reported that the complaints have been or will be taken care of. Months later there are still no results. The Ministry's response is often that the infrastructure is just not there to meet the demands. You can't make machinery, or build houses when materials are unavailable. You can't stop production and still pay people unemployment or social security in a country going broke. Convincing arguments of why things can't be done exist side by side with unnecessary failures to deliver. Knowing which is which is not always easy. Workers usually understand these arguments and they believe them, to a point. Then they say, you could do more. Unless you live here for a while, you don't see that interchange.

Not long ago, we got a complaint about a pesticide hazard. Three of us went out. The workplace was in the middle of one of the biggest labor disputes in the country. The cotton grower had fired two of the main organizers for the ATC Union and was making an agreement with a very small anti-Sandinista union. The workers were split. What impressed me was that the inspection went ahead despite the union certification dispute, and that the Ministry had enough trust in me to put me into this somewhat delicate conflict. I would have thought they would have either held me back or waited for the pesticide inspection until the union dispute was resolved. Instead, they handled it just like any other health and safety issue. We found some hazards, but not many serious ones. We reported the necessity of eliminating the possibilities for pesticides splashing about when being mixed. At the same time the airstrip itself was one of the cleanest I've seen, and I reported this to the employer–the head of the right-wing business association COSEP–and the Ministry.

Democracy here is such that every syndicalist and political point of view must undergo the test. They must convince people they have something to offer them. The marxists along with capitalists and everybody else have to line up. For example, I was recently at a furniture factory, and the Marxist-Leninist Popular Action Movement (MAP)–who preach Socialism Now, wanting only workers in power–was holding a meeting with about 40 workers on their lunch break. The guys addressing the workers were dressed like academics. One was referred to as "doctor." He stood out like a sore thumb. The other one was every bit the film character: humorless, sunken-eyed, young university student. The interaction was at once heated and friendly, respectful and contentious. Nobody seemed particularly concerned that I was there. The MAP people said they favored the FSLN program but thought that the FSLN-led government had betrayed the program. MAP wants to put the revolution "back on its true course." A number of workers thought that sounded rhetorical and they shouted Sandinista slogans. One worker retorted that Sandinismo was born in the mountains in the midst of a struggle to free Nicaragua, and that the philosophy of the Marxists was born in another part of the world in another century and didn't belong here. The guy was no FSLNer and in his fifties. But he firmly believed the FSLN was the party that represented his interests as a Nicaraguan and a worker.

The MAP and their small workers union, FO (Workers Front), did play a positive role during the insurrections. They had a military section and many of their members died. But right after the triumph, they organized almost daily strikes against private and state-run companies. At that point, the FSLN cracked down on them. Their point being this was not the time to shut down production with the country literally in ruins. And the election results confirm their limited support. While the FSLN received 67 percent of the vote, MAP hardly earned one percent. (See Appendix I)

(Six months after the triumph, the government stopped MAP's daily newspaper, El Pueblo, from publishing, and arrested some of the leaders. After a trial found them not guilty of subversion, they were released. One co-director is back teaching philosophy and participating in state affairs, the other co-director is a high ranking official in the Ministry of Interior. MAP now circulates periodicals, and still complains that the bourgeoisie can publish daily newspapers while they can not. Recently, they won the right to do so but lack the funds at this juncture.)

Q. How do you compare the health and safety conditions of the private and State-run operations?

Some of the worst I've seen are State-owned farms. State farms were either holdings of Somoza and his cronies or were allowed to deteriorate (often part of the process known as decapitalization) while in private hands after the Sandinista victory. Either of these reasons led to these farms being nationalized into State farms. This helps explain why these particular farms pose unusually high risks for workers. The

Somocistas were not known for maintaining safe conditions on their farms, so the State inherited high risk work places. Decapitalization means that most equipment is allowed to run down and safety equipment, wash facilities and the like, are not provided.

I've seen just as bad safety conditions in private enterprises, too, but on the whole private companies have more resources, modern equipment, and some have a longer history of operating. This tends to make them a bit safer. Overall, though, the workers at State-run farms and cooperatives are more aware, better organized, and tend to assert themselves more. Safety complaints are lodged in proportionately greater numbers from these workers.

It is only since the revolution began that there has been any enforcement of health and safety codes. It is the first time the State has trained and sent out inspectors regularly. But it is too soon to see much result. There is no accumulative data to compare. Yet I've seen little things. They did a survey of all the plants in the nation where noise is a problem. Hearing loss is a major occupational hazard because there are all these old machines with worn parts that clatter and clang. Because the survey was done, a union in Seattle was contacted and donated earplugs. I went to the ceremony with all the factory union representatives attending. Something like 5,000 earplugs were handed out. This is great solidarity and helps in the short run, but the machines need replacing or redesigning for longer term results.

Q. Do you hold a critical attitude toward the revolution?

It is difficult to consciously criticize the process because when I do, I learn why such and such was or was not done, and the reasoning is logical. For instance, it is easy to be against censorship. But when you look into what is really going on here, you wonder what else could be done. *La Prensa,* for instance, is purposefully provocative with the motivation of wanting to be censored. It plays to an international audience, not to

85

Nicaraguans. It constantly manipulates facts, taunting, creating fears. They don't just print distortions, they flat out lie. And that is even with censorship.

Yet it is a hazard not to express criticisms of the revolution. I am a critical person by nature. I am no blind cheerleader. What I have found due to my critical attitude is that whatever mistakes leadership makes, the potential is always there to correct them, to make a positive impact on our lives. That is what is so appealing. That is why we should contribute whatever we can to help this country, this revolution. If we don't, we will have lost yet one more opportunity.

Q. How do you feel working at MITRAB, one of a kind?

The Ministry of Labor is a real interesting place to be. Our minister is one strong reason. There has been a recent change, and I find it pleasant. The former minister, Virgilio Godoy, is a lawyer by profession. He resigned his post to run for the presidency on the PLI ticket (PLI-Independent Liberal Party won ten percent of the vote). Godoy's personal style is that of an academic: aloof, well-dressed by middle class standards. I never met the man, though I worked for him for a year. I don't think he was a bad minister, and most respected him and the work he did. The new minister, Benedicto Meneses, was a combatant, a front-line officer under Edén Pastora. He's a hulk of a man. He dressed in blue jeans with a two-inch cuff rolled up and a cotton plaid shirt. He hangs out in the hallways and talks with everyone. Benedicto looks like a bearded lumberjack without suspenders. He gives a distinct and healthy personality to the Ministry. It feels like a ministry of labor under him.

I work with inspectors who are mostly young, recent graduates of university courses. They are out-going people, thoughtful, and most are commited to the revolution. They play around a lot, and joke with me, the only "gringo" in the place. I feel accepted.

Last week, I was at a birthday party for one of the guys. Before that, I attended the wedding of one of our women workers. The birthday celebration was for Licho, whom I feel close to. His father worked in a sugar mill all his life, and the family home is right across the street from the mill. Licho used to work in the dangerous pressure-vessel section, and now he is responsible for inspecting it. I grew up totally different, middle class United States, but Licho and I are bound together because we work for the same thing. When we do an inspection, we are there to solve the same problem for the mutual benefit of Nicaraguans, and in a larger perspective, eventually for humanity. Ideas and work unite people, creating lasting friendships. Licho took me home with him over a two-day period. I got to see how his family lives across the street from this noisy mill with soot from the smoke stack settling over their yard. Everyone's life revolves around the mill's schedule. Licho's father worked his way up to become a leader of one section of a floor, but was frequently thrown out on his ear because of his union activities. When the triumph happened, he went into semi-retirement as a part-time watchman at the plant. His family feels secure now.

I'm happy working here. I feel alive.

(Doug's borrowed pickup, jammed with inspectors on their way to a blood sampling operation for pesticide poisoning, was suddenly engulfed with the foul smell of insecticide gas. I looked out to see a flagman standing knee-deep in cotton, waving to a circling airplane. It banked and flew in low, spraying pesticide over the plants and the flagman. Doug wrinkled his nose and said, "Reminds me of Ernesto Cardenal's poem about the triumph, 'Lights.'"

That top-secret flight at night.
We might have been shot down. The night calm and clear....

The Milky Way above, and the lights of Nicaragua's revolution.
Out there, in the north, I think I see Sandino's campfire....

Now we're burning close to Leon, the territory liberated.

A burning reddish-orange light, like the red-hot tip of a cigar.
    Corinto:
the powerful lights of the docks flickering on the sea.
And now at last the beach at Poneloya, and the plane
    coming in to land,
the string of foam along the coast gleaming in the moonlight.
    The plane coming down. A smell of insecticide.
And Sergio tells me: "The smell of Nicaragua!")

He continued:

By sampling workers' blood we can detect the level of pesticide poisoning they may receive working around insecticides. We give the workers the results withing hours so they can be removed from exposure, if they have too much pesticide in their system, and get treated. If a worker must stop work for a period, his wage is paid by the social security system, new since the revolution.

Our inspection and sampling teams discuss what we have observed when we return to our offices. Our inspection today in the cotton-banana cropland of Chinandega-Leon is well integrated: Higinio is head of MITRAB's health and safety quality control section, Aquiles is its chief of agricultural health and safety—both have been mobilized in the war more than once—Cory is a lab technician with the Ministry of Health, Dr. Feliciano Pacheco is the regional department head of that Ministry's occupational health division, and Dr. Gretchen Newmann is one of a dozen volunteers I've contracted from California to help out. What I hope to achieve is greater cooperation between the ministries involved. We want to know just how high the level of poisoning is so we can best combat it. When the closed systems are installed, hopefully, we'll be able to compare poisoning levels. Our reporting system is getting better, but is still inadequate. We are learning that intoxication appears higher this year than last. We've had a reported 150 cases in this region this season. Three workers have died. In one case, I know for certain she could have survived if we'd had the right machine. The poison attacked her central-nervous system and she died of respiratory arrest. A shameful waste. The medicine she needed, Praladoxime 2-PAM, is hard to get here.

Q. Why are you getting more poisoning cases rather than fewer?

Coincidentally with this trip, Dr. Pacheco was quoted in today's *El Nuevo Diario* about the problem. He said the Ministry of Health is quite worried about the setback. In 1982, no serious cases of intoxication were reported but in 1983 there were 100 cases and four deaths. Right now 18 people are hospitalized. The reasons are due mainly to the war, plus better reporting that indicates the true picture more thoroughly. Many workers have yet to receive safety training, or have had it and forgotten. Sometimes workers feel it is too hot to wear protective clothing, other times it's not available. Many just have a habitual casual attitude about safety. Some employers are unconcerned or ignorant. We try to step up our training programs but we always lack transportation.

(We arrived at Las Mercedes State banana farm, a few kilometers south of Honduras in Chinandega. The clinic is a wooden house just like the workers' houses next to it. The sampling-inspection team set up shop as the women workers line up. Women do the pesticide work, throwing powdered poison around the trunk of the thick tree-like plants. The men do the heavy carrying of banana branches but most of them are out fighting contras nearby. The women in line wear shower clogs mostly, and have no special clothing, not even gloves. Dr. Newmann and Higinio write down their answers to the questionnaire. Then they stick out a finger for Cory to prick it and take drops of blood, which she immediately mixes in a solution in a test tube. Later Cory records the results and makes sure any positive results go to the worker and the closest medical clinic. Of the 55 workers tested today, none were found to have fresh pesticide

poisoning. Ten had been previously treated for poisoning. Only 15 said they had received any safety instructions regarding pesticides. The last person in the clinic is a man, one of six of the 50 tested last week who had been poisoned. The others are in combat. Cory approached Dr. Pacheco: "This man was supposed to go to the clinic last week, but he didn't get to the right place so he continued working."

Dr. Pacheco looked at the workers, than at Doug.

"OK. Let's have him go to the clinic now. Doug, I think this is sufficient evidence. We've seen this before. From now on, whenever we find any level of poisoning, let's write it down twice, making sure both the clinic and the work place adminstrator get the information. The worker must take off work and be treated immediately.")

On the return trip, I ask Doug what he sees for the future.

I feel like there is no place on earth like Nicaragua right now. You saw how one health policy got set this afternoon: right on the spot. Things happening here now have never happened before, and may never happen again. It's exciting. There is so much opportunity to solve problems here, problems that exist in other places where the opportunity to resolve them is non-existent. OSHA is a good example.

I want to stay yet I miss the United States, too. I miss little things: trout fishing, the San Franciso 49ers, Italian food, the northern California countryside, movies. I never get to go to a good movie here. I miss my friends and family. That's hard sometimes, but you can't have it all.

Living in a Third World country is something people in the U.S. should do. It would make them grow. You end up questioning what is really important, what basic needs one actually has. There are these challenges to basic assumptions we all have about ourselves and the world. We Americans have baggage we don't need. We need to live with less without being fearful that the hungry hordes of the Third World are going to take what we have and force us to live without enough. Most

Third World countries are very rich in natural resources, much of which goes untapped or when tapped it goes directly into the banks of a few corporation owners. It's amazing that Nicaraguans still like the United States. They want to share with it though, not be dominated by it. They want to make the advances they know they can that would bring them a healthy, viable existence. They want the same things people throughout our development have always wanted. And all Americans would definitely benefit if we had a peacetime economy and peaceful atmosphere. If the U.S. government could just see that and stop warring against Third World nations struggling to become autonomous, we'd all have more funds for services and useful production, we'd all experience psychological relief. Working people in the U.S. are very uptight. They live in an increasingly tense environment, largely made so by their government's belligerent stands. Look at the negative sense of any future the young people have. Half of them believe they'll die in a nuclear holocaust.

Q. What would you do if Nicaragua were engulfed in an invasion?

I would feel uncomfortable with the whole subject because I haven't worked out what I'd do. I don't see myself as a combatant. I'm more useful being a technician or bringing information to people in the United States. That was the problem in Grenada. There was no one to bring the American people the truth. But then there may be no planes flying out. I just don't know, and it's not because I haven't thought a lot about it. It's just that I feel totally confused. I don't know if I'd leave if I could or stay. The circumstances may well dictate what I'd do at the moment.

Q. How does the war affect you personally?

There is a pervasive sense that no matter what we do to improve our lives the war will destroy it. Of course that is the Pentagon's "strategy." Yet more often than not people unhesitantly go about producing while burying their dead. My housemates and I check in with each other daily, if the phones are working. We have a sense of impending disaster, and want to be sure we know where each other can be found. When the Managua airport was bombed it brought me right out of bed. I expect the same and worse at any moment.

Not long ago, the war came home to us and I was unable to think of anything else for a long time. A friend of ours was killed by the contra in the hills east of Matagalpa. I found out about Noel's murder by reading the morning paper. I saw the article but didn't read it at first: there are so many names in the papers of killed Nicaraguans. Glancing back through the story my stomach sank. The same day a friend who lived close to Noel's coffee farm called Laura to tell her the contra had tortured Noel and then beat him to death. That night I lay in bed tossing, thinking of Noel. Laura and I had spent wonderful days with Noel and his wife Gladys on their large farm. We rode horses, we hiked the hills, we swung from the lianas, those great hanging vines that grow in the rain forest. We once spent the whole night talking near where he was murdered. They are, were...such wonderful people. Gladys is from the oligarch. Her brother, Alan Bolt, is the nation's leading playwrite and theater director. Noel came from a worker's family. He and Gladys met in San Francisco, of all places. Noel was working nights in a warehouse. Gladys was visiting the city on a break from college in the east. They fell in love and returned to Nicaragua in the mid-1960s. Twenty years later they were still very much in love. She is an articulate, assertive person. He was more reserved, yet confident. They were close to their five children, and they cared more about the conditions of workers than most landowners. They built a school on the farm, and brought doctors who otherwise would not have come. One night while we were there, Noel went to town and returned with a four-piece mariachi band to celebrate the end of the harvest. He and Gladys were clearly part of the new Nicaragua. For this the contra killed him.

Somoza's national guard, then in power rather than the renegades they are now, had once come looking for Noel in

1978. They were away from their former farm when the guardsman burned it down and killed whatever farm hands they could capture. Noel never took up arms. He was a farmer, loved and respected by people. When he was found murdered he was tied up. His ribs had been broken, his fingernails torn out, and his body had been repeatedly stabbed and cut by a bayonet. Imagine the terror he must have felt.

For days whenever I tried to sleep I saw myself being tortured. This tragedy is hard to comprehend for someone raised in the relative security of the United States. I try to tell myself that this is the war. Noel was one of the several thousand who have died like that. Still, this is so much closer. I felt defeated for some time. I wished I never knew of the contra, the war, of the Noel's and Gladys's, any of it. At the same time I feel proud to have known Noel, to be living and working with these people.

(Later I met Gladys. I was with a group of U.S. farmers who were touring Sergio Amador's private 3,000 acre rice farm in the Matagalpa area and a smaller state farm enterprise. Later we were driven to one of Amador's private homes, escorted by a caravan of Nicaraguan private farmers and UNAG leaders. Gladys was among the escorts. After food was served, a mariachi band struck up gay dance music. Tears dropped gently onto Gladys' plate as she watched. She whispered to me, "I miss Noel so much. I haven't danced since they killed my lovely husband." Wanting to be hospitable, and also close to these American farmers, she insisted they come to her house for breakfast. The next morning we filled her home. A fruit farmer from California presented her with burlap sacks for carrying coffee berries on the farm she must direct alone. "It's hard for me now. I am so alone. I must be mother and father and administrator. If anything, though, I am more determined to support our national revolution," she told me. "I knew it was the United States intelligence agencies and their contra friends who murdered Noel, and not the American people. They are my friends.")

Joan Parajón   *photo: Ron Ridenour*

Joan Parajón

Jesus Would Be Happy With Nicaragua Today

Joan was born into a conservative, middle-working-class and actively religious family near Chicago. In 1956, Joan attended Denison University at Granville, Ohio where she met her Nicaraguan husband-to-be, Gustavo Parajón. Gustavo's father was pastor of Nicaragua's first Baptist Church: now there are 55. Joan graduated with a major in music and married in 1959. Gustavo attended Case Western Reserve Medical School at Cleveland, Ohio where they lived for eight years. Gustavo completed his internship, and they moved on to Harvard so he could acquire a master's in public health. They moved to Nicaragua in 1968. Joan looks like the midwestern mother and wife movie-goers imagine. She is friendly and considerate, freckled and frail, and wears red lipstick and earrings. She supports her husband's busy work life and rears her family in a warm atmosphere.

Our work began in Nicaragua with the backing of our Baptist church in Cleveland. My husband started a vaccination program in rural communities and several weeks each year young people from our church would come down to live and work in communities in Chinandega. They dug latrines, helped build clinic buildings, and gave talks on public health. This project, known as *Provadenic*, stimulated Nicaraguans to make their own primary health care programs so it wouldn't be just a summer effort. Gustavo organized it. Each community chose its own health leader who then came to Managua for training in simple treatments and rudimentary diagnosis so he or she could advise a sick person when it was necessary to see a doctor. Then our clinics came into the picture. We started with three and now we have 30.

The Somoza government didn't have anything at all like *Provadenic* so Somoza let it develop on a private basis. The decrease in sickness was considerable where we worked, and our program changed the lives of many people, even young, wealthy Nicaraguans who translated for the Ohioans on their trips. The horrible poverty was an eye-opener for them and some became rebels.

I was basically naive for a long time. I really didn't understand what was going on because of my background. I began to learn when Gustavo would tell me about some of Somoza's corruption and after I began devoting summers to hosting the Cleveland volunteers. Driving throughout the country, I saw endemic poverty that you see little of in Managua.

At the time of the earthquake, and in light of the total lack of concern by Somoza, my husband started CEPAD (Comité Evangelico-Pro Ayuda Desarolla–Protestant Committee to Aid Development). Its initial task was to help the earthquake victims and coordinate the various church donations. It was the first time that all the denominations talked together rather than bickering. They supported the creation of CEPAD. Its work has branched out since Somoza's overthrow. Now, CEPAD does lots of community work, teaching people how to build homes, improve farming methods and develop running water. There is also a small theology school and work with pastors. The Managua staff alone numbers fifty. CEPAD is still funded by church charity from the U.S. and several European countries.

Q. What do you think of the Sandinista government?

From the beginning we have had a good working relationship with the new government. We are independent from it but we meet with appropriate government agencies so we don't duplicate work. We respect each other. CEPAD has aided in getting large donations for the various vaccination programs and we work in them, too. Our efforts are small, whereas the government can reach the entire nation with consistency.

I think the government is doing a wonderful job with the limited funds and resources available. I am angry that so much money has to be wasted on defense, money that is taken away from the health and development of people. I often think about what Nicaragua would be today if there was no aggression.

Our two older children participated in the literacy crusade. Marta was 16 then, David 14. She is studying agricultural administration at the Catholic university here, and David is back at Denison University. Marta also translates and is a mother...and a widow. She was married to Edwin for nearly two years when suddenly he drowned in a freak accident. It is such a tragedy. Edwin was a lovely man and a promising Baptist leader.

Anyway, the crusade was a wonderful project. Marta and David went with a small group of 13 from the American School—it is supposed to be apolitical and teaches in English. Most of the students are Nicaraguans who hope to attend college in the U.S. Our son was the only one in his graduating class who was in favor of the revolution, and they gave him a tremendously hard time. During the crusade, I went to Chontales where David was with a poor family and Marta was with a middle-class one. David was worried he wouldn't be able to teach his "mother" and "father" to read and write but he did. He helped with the family chores, wading through mud up to his knees. Before he went on the crusade, he wasn't interested in school much, earning C grades. But when he returned, he started getting A's and B's. All of Marta's students were farmers and she taught four of them to read and write, literally by candlelight. Both kids returned home at the end of the crusade with hepatitis. A month later, Marta received a long letter from one of her students, written in nice letters thanking her for coming to teach. She was ecstatic. All the bugs, the monotonous food, the illnesses were worth it. This is one of the most successful efforts the government has undertaken despite all the lies to discredit it, contending people didn't learn to read and write. We know the truth because we participated.

It seems you have to be here to understand the truth. Hardly anyone who comes here from the States doesn't return with their life changed. My brother came recently. His eyes were opened. Back home, he'd read in the local paper that the revolution had deteriorated so badly that there was no more garbage collection. Can you imagine? I had him take pictures of our garbage trucks one morning. You see, the newspapers have really done a disservice. I don't understand how they are so controlled. What is the fear of telling the truth? Will they be closed down? A major part of our lives must be spent countering however we can the lies of the Reagan government and the controlled press. If it gets to a point where we can't work because of the United States...Stop for a moment...Excuse my emotionalism. I just don't know what our role would be if the United States were to take over again. I can't imagine it. On the other hand, I can't believe the U.S. is spending all that money in Honduras and on the contra without something big happening. How can they justify all the money if they aren't going to use it for something?

Q. How do you compare the society now with the Nicaragua you knew before the revolution?

I think Jesus would be very happy with Nicaragua today. He would certainly be outraged at the war-makers. Nicaragua comes closer to what he preached, as we read in the Bible, than the life of the U.S. society.

Nicaragua has become a much more caring society, more sensitive to the needs of people. Before, it seemed like everyone was out for whatever they could get for themselves. Luisa is a good example of the new Nicaragua. Before, she lived off the streets, selling candy from a basket she carried on her head. Since the triumph, she has been able to get a loan in order to start a little grocery store. I began buying there when a scarcity of bread and milk hit us. I discovered she had both. There was something that clicked between us, and we became good friends. She started having a hard time getting some items because of transportation difficulties. One day I told her that I had a station wagon that we could use to go the long distance to buy certain items. She hesitated. I insisted. For a long time thereafter, I'd take her once a week to the market in my air-conditioned car. Luisa's business got better and eventually she found a place closer by to buy her wares so she didn't need my service any longer. But we continued our friendship and even started trading items. She always made sure I had sufficient bread. It was easy for me to get soaps and deodorants for her and she saves things for me. The other day, for instance, Luisa moved me very much. I hadn't found eggs nor had she. But soon she presented me with two dozen. She had gone a long way to buy four dozen, and carried them all the way on the bus in order to give me half of them. That is something I never saw during Somoza's days.

Q. Do you participate in your community?

We've become friends with everybody where we live mainly because I used to be active in our local block organization, the CDS (Sandinista Defense Committee). I was chosen to be health leader mainly because my husband was too busy, I think. Besides directing *Provadenic*, he is president of CEPAD and preaches at the church on Sundays.

Our CDS fell apart, unfortunately. I think it will get back on its feet soon, though. Basically the problem was due to one man, a very radical Argentinian who had fought. But he was not a typical Sandinista. He wanted to condemn so many people in the area, saying they were counter-revolutionaries. No one else could see that they were and he got people angry. He was responsible for getting one man in jail and this polarized the community. The collaborator had worked in Somoza's son's office but I wouldn't say he caused any deaths. My husband helped get the man out of jail later, and he fled to the U.S.

Before the CDS fell apart, we worked on many projects and were able to get electricity and running water to every home.

Q. What is your daily life like?

Besides all the health and religious work my husband does, he also has a radio program. He makes a 15-minute daily tape for our church, which is broadcast nationwide here. So that's when my day begins. I get breakfast and get Becky, our third child, off to school. Three days a week I have a radio schedule at 6:30 a.m. I'm a ham radio operator. I talk to my two friends in Cleveland and Kansas. They want to know about Nicaragua but are not at all supportive of the revolution. I still have a lot of contacts with our home church in Cleveland so people come here and we correspond. In fact, our pastor is coming soon on CEPAD business. Then our Baptist office in Valley Forge, Pennsylvania and I keep in touch. We do many phona-missions, in which we talk to Baptist churches throughout the U.S. Churches have a telephone hooked up to their public address system, and on Sundays they call us to talk about Nicaragua and CEPAD. We get all kinds of questions. Just two weeks ago, I spoke with a church in Illinois. I told them what was going on at our church that morning. They were surprised to hear that our service is like their own, and that we have classes and services with so many people, from 250 to 300. Our sermons are always based on Biblical verses that we are studying. Right now we are on Exodus.

I am director of the choir and its organist. The choir sings on Sundays and for special programs. I sang for a year in a Boston choir, then with the Cleveland Orchestra Chorus under Robert Shaw and later with his Chamber Chorus for eight years. I also did some professional singing.

People here love to sing, but they know very little about music. In our choir of 30 only three can read music. So it requires a lot of time and effort on my part going over and over all their parts. Of course, there is no music store in Nicaragua. Our Baptist book store has more music than I saw in the rest of Central America. You can't even get music sheets. Well, I started teaching a few in the choir how to read music, but the course fell flat because the young people were too busy.

Then we have a tremendous number of letters to answer to churches that have us as their special interest missionaries. It is the custom of the American Baptists to assign missionaries to different state churches. Right now we are the special missionaries for Indiana and Iowa. There are just too many letters. They want to know what is going on down here. They say they read in the newspapers that we are living in communism and ask why we are still here. I get very upset. I know I shouldn't because they've been trained to believe what the President tells them. It wouldn't be said or printed if it weren't true, they think. Ha. Ninety percent of the people who write say that. Can you believe it? It appalls me.

After one of these phone-missions, I got a letter from a church member who said the congregation was moved by what I said and was upset with the U.S. government. Thank God. I had told them that if we were living in communism we would not have the liberties we have. Furthermore, I have never felt any kind of hostility toward me at any point. People distinguish between American citizens and the government.

Another time, a church member asked me for a personal example of how I am persecuted for my faith. I replied that never in any place at any time had I experienced persecution nor have I ever been restrained from saying whatever I felt. The hierarchy of the Catholic Church may say they are persecuted, but they do so only because they are opposed to the revolution. They have some pressure on them, no doubt. I think they *should* have something said to them. They support the counter-revolution. That priest Peña was aiding the counter-revolution directly. The government had all the evidence they needed on tape and all those explosives he was carrying in his bag, and still it let him off. Most of the pressure on the Church hierarchy comes from the grass roots. A couple of times a leading anti-revolutionary spokesman has had his windshield smashed by an irate ordinary Nicaraguan, but when it comes out in the U.S. press it is the *Sandinista Government persecuting* the opposition. It just isn't true. Everybody can say what they want and practice their religion. In communist countries Christians don't participate in the government. Here we have four top Christians in top jobs and the Church hierarchy wants them out.

They don't want us to participate in the national life. Obviously this is not communism. It is something quite different, and the United States is afraid of the example that Nicaragua is setting so they try to make people believe it's a Marxist Communist Revolution. I don't buy that. Indeed, I'd say Christian influence here is greater than Marxist influence.

Q. Aren't there Marxist-Christians?

I know Ernesto Cardenal calls himself a Marxist-Christian. But in the true sense of Marxism you can't believe in God and be a Christian and a Marxist. Ernesto likes to combine the two because he has taken from both. I say that Marxists and Christians here have learned to work together well, but that doesn't make them one.

Some people have gone to the extent of even calling my husband a communist in order to condemn his work. This started in Washington, D.C. We get all kinds of responses from church people because they read this stuff in the Washington Post and especially in publications put out by that IRD (Institute for Religious Democracy). They lump together everybody working for progress and come up with, "Those who support the revolution are Sandinistas and all Sandinistas are communists, therefore..." Our home office gets letters asking if they know their Nicaraguan missionary is communist. Some organizations have withdrawn support from CEPAD because of these lies. What we believe is all in the Bible. Sharing what we have, working with all those around us. Nicaragua's revolution is native, nationalist, and Christian. Nicaragua will no longer be a puppet, period. That disturbs a lot of Americans because it means the United States has lost control. So they try to paint it bad. Why doesn't the U.S. send people to work with the revolution instead of against it? Europeans come here to work, and so do many private citizens from the U.S.

I don't know. I guess I'm just naive. The United States–I always thought the very name connoted honesty! I've read some of Reagan's speeches. I am absolutely appalled. He mixes in all kinds of lies in order to manipulate people. That speech he gave in Ohio at the National Association of Evangelicals, for instance. He mentioned that something like 200 pastors in Nicaragua are in jail. People must think that is terrible. You see, they say, that is persecution. But it is just totally false. CEPAD would be the first organization to know if there were pastors in prison because we go to jails to defend people. If there was even one pastor in there he would certainly shout very loud and we'd know. But this high figure coming from the President of the United States scandalizes people, and it is a complete manipulation. This kind of thing has really disillusioned me. People follow him blindly just because he exudes some kind of honesty with his facial expressions, the grandfather image. You know, the man next door, your neighbor and mine. Yet all the time he is saying things that just aren't true. Whether he knows it or not, I don't know. That would really be incredible if he would just accept what aides tell him without checking. But I don't know how you beat it. It's like dealing with an octopus. It has arms everywhere. When they try to make my husband out to be a communist, they must be desperate. There is no one that has done more for the evangelical community. He dialogues with pastors. He works in health, in community services. He tries to hold it all together, showing that we must participate everywhere. That is our role as Christians. That is what Jesus demands of us: to serve our fellow man.

Q. *I want to read to you from the October 12, 1984 edition of* El Nuevo Diario, *my translation.*

"I am like you, a disciple of Christ."

He who said this is not a member of any religious denomination, nor a diligent visitor of parishes. He is Sandinista Commander Tomás Borge Martínez, Minister of the Interior of Nicaragua. "Between Christians and Sandinistas a true integration must be formed. Not a simple tactical unity, nor strategic, but a true integration. A Christian can be a Sandinista and a Sandinista a Christian," Borge said.

I agree with that. I don't see any reason why a Christian can't be a Sandinista. But that's definitely not the same thing as being a Christian and a Marxist. That is what the U.S. media always says. Big headlines: Nicaragua's Marxist Government, blah, blah, blah. They never print just The Nicaraguan Government, nor do they clarify what Sandinismo is because that's part of the washing of the brain.

Q. Do you think Tomás Borge, the reputed "heavy," the "Marxist-Leninist" founder of the FSLN, is really a Marxist?

I can't honestly answer that. I like him very much. He's one of the people I like most in the government. He is a warm, loving person. He always mixes Bible verses in his speeches. When he was in prison all those years he did a lot of Bible reading. They say he's a Marxist. Maybe he uses some things from Marxism, but I still think he has more Christian in him than Marxism. In fact, I haven't met anyone in government who is a communist, and I meet a lot of government people.

Q. How does the war affect you?

We live in constant tension, wondering when we are going to look up in the sky and see the planes flying over. Certainly, this war affects our work. We're a peace-loving people. We actively seek ways for peace and yet it is impossible with someone who is constantly promoting war. We've had to close some clinics even. In the communities where *Provadenic* works, there are about 15,000 residents, mostly resettled refugees from war zones. This past year, 20,000 patients were seen, whereas the previous year there were 28,000. That's because some clinics still functioning in the north can't send out medicines because the person who drives the jeep would be in too much danger.

Ana Julia, just 20 years old, was killed in the Río Blanco

when 20 contras–one of them blond and blue-eyed–took her out of one of our clinics. They called her a communist because she was working with *Provadenic* and CEPAD. Then they cut her throat and threw her in the river. Their message: Don't help your community because that is aiding the government. Of course, it doesn't matter to them that *Provadenic* and CEPAD are private and supported wholly by church people and church institutions. And these are contras who say they are Christians who have come to save Nicaragua from atheist communism. Ana's brother-in-law heard them from where he was hiding. He said they hunted for Ana's little 12-year-old niece, too, because sometimes she assisted her. Fortunately, she was visiting friends that day or they would have "liquidated" her as well.

We have also had CEPAD vehicles machine-gunned. In one attack, they killed a six-month-old baby and an 18-year-old boy. This is the kind of war the United States is promoting.

Q. What does it feel like being a citizen of the United States living in Nicaragua?

Nicaragua is my home. I am still a U.S. citizen and I visit there every year, but I identify with the Nicaraguans and their suffering. I feel very ashamed and very disillusioned with our government that they could be the one that's causing all the suffering here.

I made the decision when Grenada was invaded. I decided I wouldn't leave if there was an invasion. The U.S. Embassies always offer a flight out when they invade or when one of their dictators, like Somoza, gets overthrown. I decided I couldn't do that. I couldn't leave for sanctuary in the country that had caused the problems. Even though I love my family in the States and my many friends, who all offer me their homes in case of a full-scale war, I just couldn't leave. Think of all the Nicaraguans who have offered their lives. How can I say to my Nicaraguan friends, who do not have the opportunity to secure their lives, that I am going to safety? It might mean my life as it did for some Americans in Chile. But I just couldn't do it.

When I take trips to the States, I hear so much chatter about nothing: a new gadget for the kitchen, a new this and that. People don't even know where Nicaragua is, nor do they care. When will they be shaken out of their stupor? I just hope that if they don't care that Nicaraguans are being killed that they will care when their own are killed.

Marco Romero   *photo: Peter Kelley*

Frances Romero   *photo: Peter Kelly*

Romero Family

Boeing Engineer Joins Nicaragua Airline

The Romeros are a unique family of internationalists. After spending a lifetime as the dutiful servants of the corporate state, Marco and Frances took their oldest son's advice and tasted the forbidden fruit. Marco retired as a supervisor at Boeing in 1982, sold the family home, and moved the family to Nicaragua, where they bought a new home and started a new "career."

Marco was born in Puerto Rico in 1922 and was raised in a middle-class, conservative home. He attended college with a major in business administration and took ROTC training before entering the army as a lieutenant and serving four years during World War II. Afterwards, he went to Cal Tech in Pasadena, California to study engineering. He took a job with Texaco in oil field engineering after marrying Frances in 1948. Marco was recalled to serve the army for 18 months during the Korean War. He worked for Texaco 10 years before moving to Seattle and joining Boeing, where he worked for the next 22 years as an engineer.

Frances was born in Albany, Oregon in 1930, the daughter of a highway engineer. She attended college in Pasadena, where she met Marco. Frances later earned a bachelor's degree in sociology and a master's in mental health psychology from Antioch College.

Edgar, the first of two sons, was born in 1951. Growing up in tumultous times, he participated in the civil rights and anti-war movements, and worked as a boycott organizer for the farm workers' UFW Union. He majored in mathematics at college. After a stint as a teaching assistant at M.I.T., Edgar got a master's degree in mathematical logic at the University of Washington.

I grew up a patriotic, apolitical American with the contradiction that inside Puerto Rico the United States was practicing a pure form of economic exploitation. In Korea, I served with the elite all-Puerto Rican Third Division. They were little, dark and mostly non-English speaking men who fought like hell for the United States. They had their *no pasaran* slogan just like the Nicaraguans do. When there was action, a lot of men were lost because of that.

My attitude about the role of the United States began to change as the movements for social change developed in the 1960's, and as our sons brought these developments home to us. Of course, I've also always been aware, though I kept it subdued, that I am not quite accepted completely because of my dark skin and because I speak with an accent. I also saw how badly Mexican farmworkers were treated and discriminated against, even by other unionists. It is a disturbing thing, something I feel Americans have the responsibility to change. But it is hard to know how to present it to them.

The United States Army and Marines, as well as mainstream America, are so effective in grouping people in put-down categories. You know, Koreans, Japanese, Chinese, Vietnamese, Laotians, Cambodians are only "gooks." The U.S. has gotten itself trapped into sponsoring so much racism, violence and terror in the world, ultimately, it seems, to keep the world as much as possible as it is for highly profitable private investments.The American public is led to believe that all this is done in the name of freedom and to prevent the oppression and terrorism of which the socialist block is accused. Actually by comparison, the oppression and abuse committed by the communist influence is much smaller than what the United States is sponsoring and really promoting. Yet to people in the United States, the U.S. is the good guy; only communists are sinners.

Q. Did that understanding lead you to Nicaragua?

When Edgar returned from his visit, what he had to say was inspiring. Frances and I decided to go for a look. We took the trip with some old friends from Texaco oil field days. We looked around and pretty much confirmed the things Edgar was talking about. Certainly we learned of the enormous need here. We returned and thought over what we had seen. We knew we didn't want the Life of Riley or the boring retired life living in a squirrel cage. So, we took the chance and came down in August, 1982, and I started teaching mechanical engineering at the University of Central America (UCA).

We believe the U.S. is on the wrong track, and we hope that by helping this democratic revolution grow, and helping some North Americans see that it has a right to survive, we are helping put the United States back on the right track.

Another reason for coming is that I am doing something I have wanted to do for many years: I am fulfilling a sense of obligation to use my education to do something for people and not just for profit.

Q. Do you actually think the people of the U. S. will change?

I think the people of the United States have a sincere desire to be good. I'm sold on the U.S. myself: its work ethic, its virtues of efficiency and productivity. But the nation must learn restraint and humility. It must redefine the meaning of success. Big business could accept the notion now guiding policy here, that of production for the good of the common folk, and still make a good profit. Maybe some might have to live with fewer luxuries, but how many cars does one family really need? If the U.S. doesn't learn to live on less, the whole world will turn against it, and the nation will either be isolated or it will blow the world up.

Q. What is your work at Aeronica all about?

Before the revolution, Somoza owned the airline. To him the only worthwhile technicians lived in the United States so all the engineering took place in Miama. Now, the State controls the airline, as it does all of Somoza's former property, and is developing its own technicians. Much of my job is teaching, on-the-job training. I joined the small technical department and now

I run the technical group. We help guide and control maintenance and quality control. We help forecasting and record keeping. We are gradually upgrading quality control for better safety and economy. I fly around the country quite a bit. We boast that not since the triumph have there been any serious accidents. Even though our planes are old no one has died from an accident. Some clients complain about scheduling, though. Since we have only ten planes, and limited resources, we often have to cancel a flight when technical problems develop. You see, the U.S. makes it hard to get spare parts and tools.

It is a bit odd to see planes from my old outfit sitting on the runway. We have one Boeing 720 and one 727, as well as a DC-3 and a DC-6, three C-46's and a Spanish turbine prop. We only have two jets. Many of our pilots are foreigners: two U.S. citizens, a Dutchman, an Argentinian and a Palestinian. Most of the pilots, including the Nicas, are not political. Many are here for the tropical climate, a bit of adventure and enjoyment in their semi-retirement. They earn well by local standards, from 12,000 to 15,000 cordobas a month. Because I work under a ministry (transport), I earn the State maximum, 10,000. But Boeing also pays me a pension.

It is very rewarding working here. People are given approval and promotion based on their degree of consistently doing good and safe work, not on the basis of rank or privilege, or who they know. I am given the feeling that my services are welcomed. I must admit that work is often frustrating. Not because of the Nicas, but because trying to run a modern airline in a country that is going broke is damn difficult. The government is seriously trying to improve communication, especially links with the Atlantic Coast. But we are so limited.

I keep busy. Besides a six-hour day at Aeronica, I still teach a class at UCA, help out with the family newsletter, sometimes attend U.S. citizen committee meetings, and I wrote a textbook for my teachings. Our family also took an active part in helping put Initiative 28 on the city ballot of Seattle, and it won. The city is now on record in opposition to the United States spending any money for war purposes in Central America, and it authorizes a city council commission to "monitor events in the region and propose further actions to the council and the mayor." Seattle is a sister city to Managua.

I've had to slow down a bit, though, recently. I just got over a bout with cancer, and my colon still gives me problems, especially when I get an attack of tropical parasites.

Q. Why did you come to Nicaragua, Edgar?

So many good people I knew were activists, hoping to improve the world at home and to stop wars. When the Sandinistas won, I was eager to come and see what they would do. I visited Nicaragua in 1981, and had interviews at the Ministry of Planning and the national university. They encouraged me to complete my master's in math and return to teach. Ironically, two math department members had just returned from a tour of U.S. colleges looking for North American mathematicians to come and teach. They didn't find anyone, which is predictable. At placement offices at graduate math programs you only see people interested in career research positions. There is no prestige in working at a Nicaraguan college. It was horrendous teaching at M.I.T. Students didn't want to learn; they just wanted passing grades to make as much money as they could. M.I.T. itself is just a huge resource for the military and big corporations. Pure mathematician professors delude themselves thinking they are not a part of this. They grind out engineers who make nuclear weapons and deadly chemicals. In Nicaragua, I see engineers finding ways to bring water to people and building roads. No one is thinking of building nuclear weapons. I saw that Nicaragua is a free country, one needing help. As a technologist, I–we–could offer help. I returned to the States with that in mind.

It took me a while to finish my degree and I've recently rejoined my folks here. My first days teaching at UNAN are filled with planning how to teach basic logic and getting acquainted with students and staff. The staff is mostly young and

113

inexperienced. Many are foreigners, mostly French. The biggest needs in math are just to enable people to do routine office work. Statistics, for example, is a high priority in order that good planning can occur.

Q. How did you become politically involved, Frances?

Life wasn't interesting for me as a housewife. I didn't like golf and cards. So I volunteered at the county hospital psychiatric outpatient clinic for six years. Through mental health day-treatment work, I became aware of abuses that people suffer at the hands of the government agencies. I went to work for the Seattle League of Women Voters hoping to help. But it is Establishment and intellectual rather than anything else. One of the things that moved me away from a non-political life was that by having children I had the responsibility to see that the world would be a little better when they grew up. I think anyone who has children takes the responsibility to raise them well—give them the opportunity for a good education and so on. An extension of that is to try to make the world a decent place for them as they grow up.

We knew people who had so much, and were so bored with what they had. Then there are so many who don't have enough. Why does there have to be that much division? When we visited Nicaragua, we saw so many really poor people. We talked with some women who had lost their relatives in the war of insurrection and later in the U.S.-backed counter-revolution. Yet these people had hope. They knew what they were fighting for. It struck me strongly. I remembered so vividly when Marco went off to Korea and left me and our small baby, Edgar. We didn't know what he was going there for.

Q. What kind of work are you doing with your psychology skills?

It took me some time to transplant our home and learn Spanish adequately so I haven't been working that long. I've seen a lot of the country and the new developments. The pride of the people is one of the most impressive aspects. I've traveled in other Latin countries but never experienced such proud people. A good example is what happened at a school I visited. It was being used as a shelter for evacuees from a flooded area. I started nonchalantly taking photos without asking anyone, a normal tourist act. One peasant refugee walked right up to me and asked what I thought I was doing. She startled me. I was both embarrassed and pleased. "Little people" don't behave like that; they submit to our insensitivities.

Another aspect of revolutionary life here is the collective spirit. Psychologists in the United States study the individual and, as such, study individualism. We are trained that outsmarting the next person, for instance, is positive, a goal for all. Now, not everybody can outsmart everybody else by definition. So most of us become frustrated and feel inadequate, and many end up on psychiatrists' couches. In the New Nicaragua, people are working for the common good and are much happier, even if they are not rich nor their egos spotlighted. Nor are the people afraid of the government as they once were. They don't shy away from criticizing or participating as the U.S. individual does. Nor are government opponents fearful of being persecuted for criticizing. People who say they are afraid only play to the U.S. orchestra. It's funny, the people who claim fear and persecution do so with great gusto as the network cameras are rolling.

After a few weeks observing, I began volunteering at the School of Special Education, the only school of its kind here. No public institution for the retarded existed before the triumph. Out of the 500 disabled children, about 100 are deaf, another 20 are blind, and most of the others have some form of serious learning disability or retardation. Some are attending who don't really belong because they are merely illiterate. That is one of the things I'll be working on, getting everybody retested because some have been misclassified. The staff is all new and few are trained. I'm preparing simple behavior modification techniques for the teachers. Many of the children with behavior problems could be corrected with such techniques. Due to a lack of methods and materials, not a lot is accomplished in education. However, they do a good job of socializing the children. They are given love and positive attention. No one is locked up.

Q. *Do you think the people of the United States will change to take an active role in what their government does to other people, and to themselves?*

I can't really answer that. I wish I could. There is so much ignorance and contentment with being ignorant. I still sympathize, though, with people who don't believe their government really acts as it does in the world. The media doesn't help much. What we saw convinced us to do something. It was hard to give up our home, and it was something of a gamble. Since we've come, we are more impressed with what we see, with what the government here is doing. At the same time, we get more depressed at what we see developing in the United States. It's a lot harder to reach Americans with what is actually going on than it is to reach poor Nicaraguans. People here are aware of their ignorance and are actively working to overcome it. But people in the U.S. are not aware of their ignorance or do not care. Many think that the truth is really just communist propaganda. What's really happening is that Nicaraguans are opening their eyes and seeing they don't have to be miserably exploited. God, I wish Americans could see that.

We put out a newsletter to help. The University-Unitarian Church of Seattle mails it to almost one thousand people now. We call it the Romero newsletter.

Q. *How long do you plan to stay in Nicaragua?*

Indefinitely. We thought through what we would do if the United States invaded Nicaragua when it took over Grenada. We decided we'd stay as long as we are welcome and useful.

116

Paul Rice   *photo: Ron Ridenour*

Paul Rice

I Was Always a Rebel

Paul Rice was born in Dallas, Texas in 1960. His childhood was spent in small towns in Texas and Tennessee following the early death of his father when Paul was only two years old. After his older sisters went off to college, his mother returned to school and eventually obtained a doctor's degree in psychology. Paul acquired diligent work skills as a youth, mowing lawns and working on a paper route and in his school office. He also earned scholarships to private schools and worked his way into Yale, graduating with a bachelor's degree in 1983.

I don't know why but I was always a rebel. Unlike all my white friends, I had Black friends. In 1976, I worked for Jimmy Carter for President in my high school where Gerald Ford got 83 percent of the student body simulated vote. DSOC (Democratic Socialist Organizing Committee) attracted me because it was against racism and war. In college, I worked in DSOC and studied political science and economics. Reading Marx, I began to see what was wrong with the world, just how it is that so many people are poor while a few are ridiculously rich.

My mother had a chance through the U.S.-China Friendship Association to visit China in 1979. I went with her and fell in love with China. When I returned to school at Yale, I studied Chinese and the great big experiment called socialism. The society that I saw, which is not necessarily the society that exists, is a society that had eliminated exploitation, one in which people worked together to solve common problems rather than working against each other. I decided to take a year off from school to live and work in China. In Peking, I studied Chinese for three months;

then I sought and was offered a job with *Peking Review* as a translator for the foreign language press. I went into China like the new kid on the block who wants to change all the rules on the first day. It took me a while to learn the ropes of the game and to couch every criticism with five compliments. I ended my year in China learning about bureaucracy, gaining some patience and shedding illusions.

Q. What was your daily life like?

Basically, I wanted to be Chinese for a year. That's not an easy goal, especially for a big nose (occidental). I lived with a family, which is also rare for a foreigner. I kept away from the foreigner haunts, wore Chinese clothes and glasses. In order to see more of China, and get away from the Chinese intellectuals, too, I met someone who lived on a commune and I rode my bike there on weekends to do physical labor with a worker-peasant team. I worked in a machine shop, harvested rice knee-deep in mud, milked cows, and did whatever the Chinese did. I learned valuable lessons, which have stood me in good stead in Nicaragua.

Because I knew Chinese and could visit most of China's provinces, I learned a lot about the working class. I also began to realize that socialism was being destroyed in China. I witnessed with sadness the opening of so-called "free markets" and speculation, the re-introduction of exploitation in which individuals can control hiring and firing and wages of many workers.

In a fundamental way, China today is not so relevant for revolutionary struggles in the Third World because the struggle now is between those who are re-introducing capitalism and those who are trying to prevent that, trying to uphold the working class democratic gains the revolution won under Mao. For communists of my generation in China, the fundamental revolutionary question is how to make and solidify socialist democracy, how to prevent the vanguard party from diverging from the interests of the masses.

I think that the Chinese leadership has reversed the developing socialist process for now, but socialism did not fail. The fact that I could sit down last summer—during my revisit to study agrarian reform—with a bunch of peasants on the inner-Mongolian plain and hear them talk about the bourgeoisie and the party, and the need for another revolution, represents the true spirit of socialism.

Q. What led you from China to Nicaragua?

By the time I returned to Yale again, I considered myself a Marxist-Leninist. I think Marxism is the best guide to action for changing the world, to bringing the working class to power so that we can stop getting shafted. I was following Nicaraguan revolutionary events the best I could from afar. The triumph occurred while I was in China. I was interested because it seemed there was a genuine and unique revolutionary process underway. The Chinese didn't make much comment on the Nicaraguan revolution then. They were critical of its ties to the Cubans and Soviets. But the Chinese had introduced me to the value of collectivism. I saw Nicaragua starting an agrarian reform program and that encouraged me to come. I studied agricultural economics and visited Nicaragua in the summer of 1982 with a grant from Yale to study the land reform. I spent three months working and living on cooperatives in Chinandega province. I got jobs by simply walking up to the cooperatives and asking. At that point, there were no houses at this main cooperative where I mostly worked. We all lived in the two big barns, divided up with sacking and boards. I slept in a hammock as did the 12 families and three single men. The farm consisted of 300 acres of grazing land and grain crops. It had belonged to a Somocista who fled in 1979. For two years it ran at a loss as a State farm. Just two months before I arrived, MIDINRA turned the land over to these peasants to run it as their own cooperative. With the few mostly untrained technicos that the Sandinista had then, it's surprising that everything did not run at a loss.

I became a field worker, milked cows, collected firewood

and water, and conducted oral histories with workers. We worked fewer hours than did the Chinese. I had been used to working from dawn to six in the evening. But in Nicaragua, people knock off in the early to mid-afternoon and attend classes in adult education. At the cooperative there was no formal teacher. The best students from the literacy crusade days taught the others, most of whom had only recently learned to read and write minimally. I sat in on classes, too. I'd learned Spanish from Mexican friends in Texas. Around nightfall, we'd go to the river and bathe. The women bathed in the morning when the men went off to the fields. In the evening, people attended meetings that dealt with co-op business, the war, politics, everything. Often, there would be religious songs and parties, especially parties for children reaching their first birthday, which is traditionally considered important because so few made it to that age. I did guard duty after I was taught how to shoot an M-16.

On the weekends, I would sometimes talk with technical people in the Ministry of Agriculture. I learned how the people I worked with had traditionally lived on slopes so steep that they never used oxens or plows. They employed the same technology people were using a thousand years ago. They planted with a stick. Every two paces, they stuck a stick in the ground, dropped a seed down and kicked dirt over it. They never used fertilizers or insecticides. Before they moved on to the cooperative, erosion would wipe out their hill every three or four years and they'd have to move on. At the cooperative, techniques weren't much better in the beginning, but I saw how inspired they all were, knowing their future would be vastly improved. One of the peasants kept telling me, the revolution is a great school. I became determined to finish my degree and enroll in this great school. So here I am.

Right off, I got a job and found a family to live with. To my dismay, however, the father was a reactionary. He hated the Sandinistas. He worked for years in customs, and I suspected he was a reactionary because he couldn't get the bribes he had before. Besides that, he was an alcoholic. He'd come home drunk and be abusive. The wife, on the other hand, was starting to break her chains. She was basically a housewife, and took in some sewing work. Her husband demanded she stay at home, but she did little things to improve her status. She struggled to get him and the kids to wash their plates, and went to some AMNLAE meetings and Christian base community meetings, too. That was really great for her. The kids are all activists in the Young Sandinistas so the house is full of conflict. I'd wake up at 5:00 or 5:30 in the morning to sounds of them shouting at each other. While I was there, two sons joined the army. One came back and told me enough war stories to last a lifetime. He and I became tight. I learned a lot, trying to be part of that family. I had to leave, though, when my compañera came to visit me from the states. Neither the man nor the woman would allow us to stay together. So we moved in for a while with some young Sandinistas I'd met at militia meetings.

Q. Why are you in the militia?

I joined the militia because I had come down just three weeks before the invasion of Grenada. When that happened the feeling was strong that the U.S. would invade Nicaragua, too. So there was a huge mobilization of civilians to train or retrain in militia exercises. Our neighborhood, Colonia Centro America, had one of Managua's 36 battalions. It was really cool. Our nightly militia sessions were drawing from 300 to 500 people. That lasted for many weeks. People worked their day and then put in three hours night training, plus long day marches on the weekends. We marched to our posts that we were to defend. We dug trenches, went through maneuvers, learned commands, fired on imaginary targets. It was not just a bunch of kids having fun. People of all ages and backgrounds joined up: grannies, workers, pre-teens. We fired live rounds. I did well since I used to hunt quail and deer in Texas. I was one of the vanguard so I got to carry the flag when we marched sometimes. Another gringo from Salt Lake City was with me. He'd never fired a rifle before and nearly shit in his pants when he fired the AK. You know there is a strong recoil. But he hit the target after a while, even though it was 500 meters off.

I came here for the revolution so I try to integrate myself in the process as far as a foreigner can. Both from the standpoint of wanting to defend the revolution and from a personal standpoint–wanting to defend my own fucking life–to me the militia is an obligation. No one wants to go off in the mountains and kill people and lose their own lives, but the point is if the Marines come that's what is gonna happen, they're gonna die. Me and plenty of others like me are going to defend this place. Everyone has the right, the obligation, to defend themselves. It doesn't matter who invades, Marines or not, we're going to kill people. At the same time, everybody here is working their butt off to prevent an invasion.

It's sorta weird. I consider myself kinda brash: I'm not real scared being down here. On the other hand, there are all kinds of pressures. Someone could do a fascinating PhD dissertation on the psychological effects of these pressures, the psychology of living in Nicaragua in these times. I've had all sorts of fantasies about what it would be like, what I would do in an invasion. I've got two high school buddies in the Marines right now. I've had dreams at night that I meet up with these guys on the battlefield. They're on the other side of the trench, and I can see them, and we are shooting at each other. It's hard stuff. But the truth of the matter is that every time I kill 'em. I know that's the way it has to be.

Nicaraguans are working to break their chains by living through this process of liberation. The United States government policy, and what a U.S. invasion would mean, is to reimpose the chains. The poor, dumb fuckers in the Marines who will be sent down here to shoot Nicaraguans, my high school buddies, are not reactionaries. They are not the ones who formulate policies. The tragedy of it is, though, they're the guys who are forced to pull the trigger, to kill people and be killed.

Q. Why do they carry out the policy they do not formulate if they are not also responsible?

You know what economic conscription is, man. You know what it's like in the inner cities. The soldiers and Marines are not the primary contradictions. They are not class enemies. They can be educated. True, as individuals they are responsible for their actions, but you know what the society is like with its propaganda machine.

Q. Is that your job, to gather material and write information to counter that propaganda machine?

Yes, partly. I do economic research for INIES (Nicaragua Institute for Social-Economic Research). Most of what I do comes out in English and goes to the peace movement in the States. I'm helping Joe Collins now with an update of his 1982 book, *What Difference Could A Revolution Make,* put out by his Institute for Food and Development Policy. It's the best thing I've seen on the agrarian reform and Nicaragua's new food policy. I'm also doing research along with others at INIES that the Ministry of Planning doesn't have the luxury of doing because it is so caught up in the crisis management involved with the war and immediate economic problems.

INIES is a private non-state institute that receives funding from many "respectable" foundations in the U.S., Europe and Latin America. It is also pro-revolution. It does research with a long-range solution perspective. One of its main ideas is the possibility of regional (Central American) alternatives to the status quo economy. We all live in a regional economic crisis and if we could combine our economic resources, we could provide the basis for long-term growth and development. Obviously, that is premised on regional liberation and peace. The idea comes from the old Central American Common Market in the 1960's, then controlled by U.S. multinational companies. Most of the industries they started were geared for luxury consumption, mainly for export-import items for the rich. But there were a few useful ones such as the chemical industry. Recognizing that Nicaragua's internal market is too small for any significant-sized chemical industry, it could function and grow if aimed at a regional market. It could take advantage of certain economies of scale, and the whole region would sensibly profit. El Salvador, for instance, could make textiles and the two countries could exchange products for mutual benefit. Of course, Nicaragua wants Central America and not the United States to control the industry and profits. So INIES provides some of the analysis, data and structural roots of economic problems and conceives possible solutions.

What we see in the past two years of Nicaragua's economic life is the sad effects of the imposed war. It's the key obstacle to eliminating hunger and establishing a firm process of growth. The war-makers have actually taken on the food sector as their key military target. Despite all the efforts that have been made to increase production, all the incentives and improved expertise, the state is only collecting half the basic grains needed for the nation. The contra mines country roads in order to destroy food transportation vehicles. They won't only kill anyone working the fields. A lot of people are talking out their ass about scarcity when they blame the Sandinistas. Well, what do they say when the bodies of workers and volunteers are brought home riddled with bullets and bayonet slashes because they were trying to bring home beans and rice to the people? It brings the whole thing down to earth.

In spite of the war destruction, Nicaragua's economic production figures grew last year while its neighbors fell backwards. The 1983 figures were better in every basic grain than in 1977, the average year under Somoza's dictatorship. Rice and sorghum were double the best year under Somoza. Beans were up 55%, corn up 30% over the Somoza high. Coffee is pretty much recovered, sugar is doing well, but, partly because of the reluctance of many rice and cotton growers to invest, cotton is way low. Many cotton growers support the counter-revolution. Yet some also work well with the Sandinistas. The bottom line of the agrarian reform is if you produce, your land won't be touched. Growers get price incentives, tax breaks, and a low conversion rate for dollars. Cattlemen, in fact, get credit at low interest rates for their production investments. The capitalist is not risking anything today. I've had conversations with many who tell me they're making more money now than ever before.

I was row boating one day on Lake Nicaragua and bumped into Alfredo Chamorro, a member of the powerful Chamorro family, which owns vast lands and *La Prensa*. He's typical of the Nicaraguan bourgeoisie. Educated in the United States, he relishes speaking English. In flowery terms, he speaks to foreigners about how much he loves the United States. He says it's the greatest land in the world and his second home. He reminds me of a Southern country gentleman: tall, white-haired, a distinguished, genteel man. He invited me for a drink at the bar overlooking the lake. He told me he would like the anti-Sandinista and contra leader, Alfonso Robelo, for president. But when he talked about his rice farms and cattle in the prime agricultural Grenada lands, he told me flat out he was making more money than at any other time. Ironically, he lost one of his farms in 1982 for failure to produce and the government got it back for him. One of the new agrarian reform laws says you can't be away for more than six months and not produce or your land will be confiscated. He took off for one of his Miami vacations and his workers denounced him to the union, saying he'd abandoned the land. The workers basically wanted the land and MIDINRA expropriated it. Old Alfredo comes back and discovers he has one less farm. He took his case to the Agrarian Reform Tribunal, set up as an appellate court when the reform laws were passed, and proved that he'd just been on vacation. The court returned his land. The guy was real pleased about that.

Q. How do you feel working at INIES?

INIES has a large staff but we get close to one another. Everyone is clear that the revolution is worth defending, no matter what criticisms one may have. There is no competitiveness, no sense of possessiveness that so many intellectuals have in the U.S. We share ideas and information. It's a good atmosphere. I did research for the department of political science at Yale. There was no way in hell you could get anyone in other research projects to cooperate with you. Every professor has his little private project that he guards with his life.

Q. What is your neighborhood CDS like?

CDS is a national organization of neighborhood committees with half a million people working in common to solve local and national needs: food distribution, garbage pick-up, pest control, health vaccinations. It's an immense organ of *poder popular* (popular power), and I participate where and when I can.

Low prices for basic foods, which the CDS administers along with a government agency, have kept the rate of inflation for the average person way down. While the overall rate of inflation last year was 40 %, for basic goods the inflation rate was only 9%. So the ratio of inflation for the majority compared with their increase in wages is roughly equal. Thus, the Nicaraguan worker is less pinched than workers in any other Central American nation, and that considering the nation is at war when its neighbors on both borders are not. In fact, Honduras' and Costa Rica's economies are propped up by U.S. subsidies.

The CDS takes house censuses in order to determine what each family's quota for the 10 basic goods should be. Ration cards are given to residents and a popular inspector is elected who ensures that the private markets' prices on these items are correct. If there are grievances, they are taken to CDS first. This ensures organized input for anyone. People in our neighborhood were used to going to the supermarket and buying weeks' worth of groceries at one time. With the new system, with the small distribution posts, you have to buy weekly. For our community, which is comprised of skilled workers and teachers who could afford to shop once a month, weekly shopping is an inconvenience. Many complained and wanted the distribution outlets to stock more goods. Our CDS met and investigated the matter. We found that the center can't stock any more since they have neither space nor funds for such quantities. The report was reluctantly accepted although people weren't happy with the reality. Unlike ever before, people at least know why things work as they do.

I worked with others to dig bomb shelters, particularly for the kids. Our CDS members dug at night with lanterns, often until 1:00 in the morning. It brought non-Sandinistas and Sandinistas together. Bombs don't discriminate. We've also organized blood drives for defense. Volunteers for the national campaigns are organized through the neighborhood CDSs with many having to travel long distances to help out. A checklist of all block residents is matched with those getting vaccinated against diseases, another CDS effort. Those not coming to the clinic are contacted by CDS volunteers to see if they can help get them vaccinated. In our CDS, we got 100% vaccinated last time.

I do *vigilancia* (night guard duty), too. An older man, a construction worker, and I do it together. His son is fighting in the army now. They are both dedicated to the revolution. In our CDS area, we haven't had one incident during *vigilancia,* but in the war zones there are problems and tensions. I've done *vigilancia* in Ocotal, in the north, and we do it with guns.

Q. How does the war affect your personal life?

For some time I worked afternoons with others at INIES digging bomb shelters, and some of us do weekend volunteer coffee picking during the harvest season. That's cool, but it's rough if you are there for three or four months straight without beds and showers. Next time, I want to go with the militia to guard the harvesters. Last year, one of my neighbors was killed picking coffee. The brother of one of my roommates was killed defending Somoto at Christmas time. My compañera and I went to the family house up north. It was no Merry Christmas. There were prayer services every day and daily visits to the grave. Even though I'm an atheist, I sat through all those prayer meetings. Our participation brought us close. It meant a lot to the mother. It was like a reaffirmation that her son had not died for nothing, having people there from the country whose government had killed her son.

I came here with the idea of staying three years. But, because of the war, I want to stay until it's over. I don't know, though, if I'll always be at INIES. I feel frustrated being an intellectual living in Managua when so much of the country is at war. I feel like being in the north, directly helping with defense needs, and living like the people there are forced to live. I love the countryside also, and feel it's healthy to work directly in production rather than in an office full of books and computer equipment. Anyway, I'll be here doing whatever I can. My contribution is just a drop in the bucket, just one piece in the millions of pieces that come together to produce this great revolutionary process. Nevertheless, my little piece is important to me so I want to stick with it as long as I can. It has nothing to do with guilt. The war-makers have nothing to do with me. I am not responsible for their actions. I know that I will spend my life fighting the imperialists, the exploiters. Ironically, perhaps, I don't hate America. Inexplicably, I feel pride in my country. I am an American. I hope one day to return and work with those who are struggling to wake up our country, to change it. That is my dream.

Q. Do you think that is any more than an unreachable dream? Don't you think that Americans generally feel that they have it good because countries such as Nicaragua have it bad?

No. I'm not convinced of that. Getting the U.S. off the backs of other countries doesn't mean the U.S. working people are going to suffer. Quite the contrary. Ending imperialism and transforming social conditions in the U.S. will give the working people a better shake than they have. It may not be clear to most of them now, but it'll come. Perhaps not until my grand-children's day, but one day.

I mean there are positive elements, many who are eager to

fight for change. But people don't know what to do. There is no analysis, no party to tell people what to do that makes sense. Sure, there's community and solidarity work, but where is it going? My feeling is that until we have a real vanguard all of our efforts are going to be guess work. We just do what we *feel* is right, and do it as *individuals,* without knowing if it's pushing the nation forward with the kind of changes a just society must make.

Q. The U.S. owns or controls about 60% of the accumulated wealth of the entire world. A lot of that wealth is there because it is robbed from places like Nicaragua. Now, if the big steal ends, if imperialism is defeated as countries win their liberation, that will mean the U.S. as an aggregate whole loses some of the wealth. The pie becomes smaller. Will Americans as an aggregate whole accept that?

I don't know for certain, but I know they don't need to have so much wealth nor lose much either. I haven't figured out the blueprint for socialism in the United States, but it seems clear that U.S. capital doesn't have to go abroad to do useful things or to create growth. Investments can be poured into improved housing, transportation, social services and to de-centralize urban over-crowding. That is the problem with U.S. capitalism now. The logic of endless, spiralling profits cannot afford a mass transit system that works. It's not profitable to individual capitalist companies. In a socialist America, It would both be useful and possible because profit is out of the picture. People throughout the world would be better off, including the currently skeptical Americans. So that is the fight I will undertake one day in the future when this war is won for Nicaragua's freedom.

Mary Hartman

photo: Lary Boyd

Mary Hartman

Jailers With Compassion

Born in the small Pennsylvania town of Altoon in 1928, the daughter of a railroad mechanic, Mary Hartman grew up with a desire to serve the poor through church work. At 20 she became a St. Agnus nun. In 1962, Mary volunteered for missionary work in Nicaragua. Those who know her well respect Mary for "her selflessness and dedication to the dignity of man," says Maria Zuniga.

My Mother Superior told us that ten percent of the St. Agnus nuns were to do Latin American evangelical work. The only qualifications were a college degree and to be stable. I had the degree and big feet, if that meant stability.

Q. How long do you think you'll be here?

I expected to be in Nicaragua five years. That was 23 years ago. I expect I'll die here. When I arrived, I was unaware of the real world. Nicaragua has taught me about the world, as well as to be generous in my vocation and to seek change when life is miserable.

Q. What has taught you these lessons?

In the beginning, I taught well-to-do kids at the Christian Brothers LaSalle School. I instructed in art, music and English, while I was learning Spanish. In those days they just sent you out with no preparation. The next year I lived among the poorest of people in Central America, the Miskito natives of Río Coco. I spent 18 months with them in the immense underpopulated Zelaya region. The Catholic Church traditionally worked through

133

occasional missions in some of the less populated areas. We visited then rather than actually living with the people. This changed after the 1968 Bishops meeting at Medellín, Columbia, after which Christian base communities were started. But even in 1963 and 1964, I saw enough of native life to be overwhelmed with the poverty. I saw people living in sub-human conditions. They knew of no other life. I think that helped them to be passive. I never expected any change.

During those early years, I would give pastoral courses to people whose poverty and passivity held me to the traditional views of the Church: the poor you will always have with you; God loves them; hold on and someday you'll get your reward. All we did was distribute barrels of food, clothing and medicine. There was never enough, but we kind of felt that we were doing good. Looking back, I would say that our visits were a distraction for the people. There were no movies or anything like that, and they had nothing to fear from us in that we were peacemakers. They also had nothing to gain from us. Our relationship to them was paternalistic.

It wasn't until after Medellín, and when I moved in with the poor in Barrio Riguerio, that I began to have hope for change. I worked through the people's church of Father Uriel Molina (Santa María de Los Angeles) on the Medellín principle: incarnate yourself into the lives of the poor and help liberate them from poverty. I realized we'd done nothing before, only applying band-aids. At best, we'd offered comfort for the poor trapped in their misery. Through Biblical circles developed at the people's church, participants for the first time began to read and interpret the Bible, and I began to feel part of the people.

At one of those meetings one of the students who was also living with the poor talked about how the U.S. powers exploited people, how they robbed Nicaragua and elsewhere. I balked at that. My idea of the United States was that we were just good buddies to everybody. This session with Luis Carrion was the beginning of a real eye-opener for me. I protested, saying that he just didn't know the U.S. He smiled and kept on explaining. I had a number of conversations with Luis about this. He'd show me documents about U.S. interventions and how the U.S. gained profits through controlling other nations. I don't see him much anymore because he's so busy in his role as one of the nine commandantes and Vice-Minister of the Minstry of Interior. But we meet occasionally, and he still teases me about that time.

Before the 1972 earthquake, three of us nuns lived in a small two-room place without any amenities. I remember the earthquake vividly. That day some ladies had come to wash the church in preparation for putting up the Christmas crib. Everything was so clean, so nice. That evening we went to the Cathedral to offer support for university students who were on a fast, seeking visitor rights for prisoners. In the late evening we received a warning, a tremor. No one paid any attention. We were all sound asleep at 12:30 when the earthquake struck. I woke up with Nancy on top of my bed. The walls fell down. The bathroom disappeared. That same day we had changed rooms. What had been our bedroom collapsed. It would have been fatal for us had we slept there.

We managed to climb out of the remaining part of the building, and we were standing by the church patio when the second quake hit. Our whole house and the church fell down like paper. One of the university students, Alvaro Baltodano, climbed up on the rubble of our home and succeeded in rescuing some of our clothes. Today, Alvaro is head of Nicaragua's militia.

The next morning we were told that any aid would come from one of Somoza's homes which is now the Ministry of Culture. Aid poured in, but it was tightly guarded and Somoza himself was surrounded by United States Army troops sent from Panama bases. Much of Somoza's national guard had fled when the quake hit and the United States saw fit to protect him. If the Sandinistas had been better organized, they probably could have run him over then.

Almost no aid ever got to the people through Somoza's channels, at least no free aid. We lived on what remained of the church patio for the next three months and did whatever we could to help the injured and the refugees. One evening after

135

church services, we had a demonstration to demand aid. We were met by guard jeeps and guardia tear gas and billy clubs. These guardia later brought in donated goods, and I watched them sell the food, medicine and clothing at whatever price they asked.

Subsequent to the disaster and because of the way the people were mistreated, more and more met to discuss just what could be done. People saw that they would have to take matters in their own hands if anything would ever get done. In meetings I attended, people decided the dictatorship would have to be overthrown. No one believed it would happen in their lifetime, but they felt they had to sacrifice even their very lives so that change could happen for their children or grandchildren.

After the earthquake, I lived with a family of ten. They put up a board so that I had a private area for my bed and visitors. There was no phone, television or refrigerator. My day began at six with a mass at church. Then I'd clean house and prepare for whatever meeting we had in the evening: women's group, men's group, youth group, and Biblical group. I taught English at the Catholic university in the afternoons. That is how I earned my living. I didn't take any church pay. Our evening meetings were based on subjects the group wanted to talk about. The topics ranged from relationships between men and women to political participation. I'd prepare a short talk and we'd discuss it, maybe see a slide show, and talk about resolutions.

Somoza was jailing more and more people, torturing most of them. The guardia dragged kids out of the barrios and we never saw them again, or sometimes their bodies were left for people to find. They had their eyes torn out of their sockets often. Instead of frightening people away from fighting, they became more fortified. Somoza didn't know about the power of the people's church.

We continued our meetings after most of the university students left the city to join up with the guerrillas. I eventually had to move away from Riguerio, though, during the time of the insurrection because the family might have been in serious danger. Prisoners were being interrogated about me, about why people came to my house. The prisoners replied that I gave catechisms and personal advice to personal problems.

I saw so many Nicaraguans being killed. Man has no greater love than laying down his life. It was a great lesson to me.

Q. Were you ready to die?

I was ready to die if I had to. That is part of being incarnated with the poor. What has been started will never be stopped. People will have liberation.

Q. You knew Steadman Fagoth-Müller during this time. What can you say about him?

Yes, he was a student in one of my English classes in 1977-78. He spoke good English, Spanish, and Miskito. I was happy to see such a well-versed person from the Miskito culture. We used to talk after classes. He would speak of his hopes for the Miskito people. He said he wanted to work for his people's progress but couldn't while he lived with an army officer's family. One day I met him casually at the airport, and he asked me if I could secure a safe house for him. I knew someone who offered a room in her house. Some time later the guardia ransacked her home. In the 1973 insurrection, the son of a well-known Nicaraguan professional man was picked up. Even though César was a U.S. citizen, the Embassy personnel did nothing. Later, I met Steadman and he was anxious to tell me he'd been in jail and seen César unconscious with an eye missing. When Somoza fled, he left his files on people, including his agents, in the bunker headquarters. There it was: Steadman had been a secret service agent. Somoza had paid his way through the university, and Steadman had informed on students, including fellow Miskitos. Many of the names he turned in were of people tortured to death later on.

Q. What did you do during the final insurrection?

137

I had moved a bit away from the center and would help as a courier. I had a small car then and would transport activists and messages. I appeared innocent enough. In the last days, I lived and worked at the seminary, helping many of the 12,000 refugees. We shared what we had, including the agony of hearing the guardia planes firing and bombing people. I was so surprised it was over as soon as it was. I had thought it would go on for years. Suddenly we had won. Oh, God, it was unbelievable. We laughed and cried simultaneously. A friend said to me, "We won, we won! I lost two sons but it was worth it." That was the spirit. The utopia lasted a while, until Reagan gave the first millions to the CIA. So Nicaragua is at war again.

It is not the war Reagan pretends it to be, though. It is the war of the giant of the North. It is diabolical. It is based on lies and a controlled press so the people in the United States won't know what is happening. Then there are also some who tolerate people being killed if they can be convinced they are "just communists." The United States is the number one country in the world, it thinks, and intends to stay that way by killing and killing and repressing and repressing.

Q. You lived through two of Nicaragua's worst historical natural catastrophes: the 1972 earthquake and the 1982 draught-flood. How do you compare how the different governments reponded to the destruction and society's needs?

That was an interesting thing to have witnessed—all the disorganization after the earthquake and how the rebuilding was just never realized. There was so much robbing and deceit. Then, with the floods, it was remarkable. The CDS organized so that people knew where to go for help. Effective relief was immediately distributed to all people. People who lost land or their crops were given interest-free credit to start up again, even those who owned private lands and maybe opponents of the revolution.

Q. What is your current work?

Nicaragua initiated The National Commission for the Promotion and Protection of Human Rights in 1980, the first country to follow the United Nations call to establish such committees. The Commission's tasks are to investigate any claims of abuses and to legally represent prisoners who ask. I was asked to volunteer as the rehabilitation worker for the prison system and was soon put on the 12-person staff. I earn 4,500 cordabas a month and work full-time. Our commission is democratically directed by 12 civilian volunteer board members. I find the work challenging, and I enjoy it. The people in the penitentiary system are sincerely interested in rehabilitating prisoners, not in punishment or revenge.

Q. When I was here in 1978 as a war correspondent, I interviewed José Esteben Gonzáles, the former director of the private organization, The Permanent Committee for Human Rights. He served an important function, recording and reporting on thousands of human rights abuses committed by Somoza's regime. What happened to him and his committee since the Triumph?

When the final days of Somoza's regime came and the United States was trying to find any alternative to the popular Sandinista victory, Esteben was with Archbishop Obando y Bravo in Venezuela seeking a U.S. intervention. Esteben wanted its support so he could become President, but the Organization of American States wouldn't back the idea. After the captured guardia were tried by people's courts, Esteben toured Europe with a list of names of 700 people he claimed the FSLN had assassinated. He even had an interview with the Pope about this. Every international human rights group that investigated the claim dismissed Esteben's charges. Americas Watch and OAS's human rights group found that most on the list were living in Miami, others were killed during the war. About 60 were killed in the first days following the victory by outraged citizens whose relatives had been brutally murdered. The FSLN and the government denounced all vigilante actions and immediately established tribunals to try the 8,500 arrested guardsmen. Another 6,000 had fled to Honduras, Guatemala and the United States, and many of them are now warring on us again. Three thousand of those arrested were released without trial due to lack of evidence of any crimes. About 1,000 were exonerated following trials, and some 4,500 were found guilty of crimes against the people and imprisoned. Half of those have been released by now. Upon the Triumph, the new provisional government abolished the death penalty and lowered the maximum sentence to 30 years. Most of those serving sentences received from 10 to 20 years; a few murderers got the maximum. In all of Nicaragua there are now 4,700 prisoners. Of these, 2,200 are former guardsmen, 800 are counter-revolutionaries, and the rest are common criminals. Amnesties are frequently declared. In 1981, 4,000 convicts picked cotton under minimum surveillance, laying the groundwork for the open farm system. Some 1,200 prisoners, mostly former guardsmen, now serve their sentences on three open farms with no armed guards or closed fences, or on three semi-open farms.

Instead of recognizing this reality, this fundamental advance in human rights, The Permanent Committee for Human Rights serves as an annex for the U.S. Embassy. Esteben works with the far-right Christian Democrat party and flies back and forth from Costa Rica to Washington, D.C., meeting with Jeane Kirkpatrick (then U.S. Ambassador to the United Nations). His committee is almost always making vague accusations and has presented no more than half-a-dozen actual cases of abuse. I looked into one of these some time ago, the case of Luis Morales. The Esteben committee claimed State Security had locked Luis up for months without charges and had tortured him. I visited him and his family. He told me he'd been in jail only two weeks and had been interrogated a total of four hours without anyone touching a hair on his head.

There is just no comparison between this government's behavior toward human beings and that of the government the United States put in power and backed for half a century. The

140

only death squads left are those the U.S. supports. Today we have law with compassion. There is no official policy of violence against prisoners or dissidents, just the opposite. When abuses do occur, the perpetrators are punished. Some 300 employees of the Ministry of Interior are serving time in jail for various violations of law, including a few abuses of prisoners. One example occurred in Grenada. We discovered some prisoners had been kept in darkness and deprived of food. These were common criminals. We took the matter to penetentiary authorities and to Tomás Borge. The guards responsible were jailed and their names published in newspapers.

One of my jobs is to see that prisoners' requests for medical aid, recreational and educational opportunities, and visitation are met. I can go into any prison unannounced at any time and meet with prisoners alone. I make recommendations for improvements and report abuses. I can honestly say that no prisoner is denied regular visitation, regardless of his conduct. Conjugal visits are also permitted prisoners in most circumstances.

The day Mary and I visited the Open Farm, located 25 kilometers outside Managua, we walked in unannounced. We found the only official on the 75-acre farm to be unarmed and talking with Herman Lozano Robles, a large man dressed in civilian clothes. I had expected to hear he was a touring official until Mary introduced me to the former bodyguard of Anastasio Somoza. Lozano had also been a well-known torturer. Still the "disciplinarian, he had been elected prison coordinator by his 50 fellow inmates. He told me, "I was sentenced to 23 years, but I only had to serve three years inside a cell. For two years now I have worked in the fresh air, and I feel useful. We are always unguarded, even when we go to town. Seventy-five men have gone through this prison farm and only two escaped. They were pressured by family break-ups."

Lozano is a model citizen today. I think he will be released soon. If it weren't for Reagan's war, half these men would be free today. As it is, 500 captured contras, including 300 Miskitos, were granted amnesty some time ago. Everyone incarcerated is currently undergoing review because the government accepted our committee's recommendation for a "Law of Grace."

Many prisoners released use skills they've learned in prison to become productive citizens, in some cases for the first time in their lives. On the farms prisoners go through a three-month agricultural course. The men plant the trees, vegetables and fruits. What they don't eat, they sell to the highest bidder, and the profits go to the Ministry of Agriculture. Unguarded production crews rotate going to town to buy supplies and sell crops. Twice a year the men get week-long vacations with their families. In their spare time they can learn to paint–often instructed by well-known painters–write poetry, play sports, listen to whatever radio station they want, read newspapers and watch television.

I conduct follow-up on some of the men released. At first I was surprised to see the results. In most cases, if they lead an honest life, they are accepted. I only know of two examples where neighbors suffered so at the hands of the guardia that they refused to accept them back. I must admit that at first I didn't know how I could be around these people. Some had torn apart the bodies of children I knew. But this revolution is a forgiving one. The United States could learn from the Sandinistas how to run prisons, to be humble and forgiving. Nicaragua has taught me about reconciliation.

Q. Why do you think the prison system is this way today?

An important reason is that the FSLN has kept to their ideal that there would be no revenge. They meant what their slogan says: Relentless in Struggle, Generous in Victory.

Tomás Borge was cruelly tortured in Somoza's jails. He was blindfolded for months on end with his hands tied behind his back and underwent many other terrible tortures. Amnesty International charged that between 1976 and 1978, he was the most tortured man in the world. He swore this type of treatment would cease when the FSLN won. When Tomás was made Minister of the Interior and charged with constructing a new prison system, he and Foreign Minister Miguel d'Escoto visited Borge's former torturer, then in prison. Miguel d'Escoto tells the story of what Borge said to the man: "I have come for my revenge. For your hate, I give you love. For your torture, I give you freedom." The man left the country after his immediate release.

Borge knows that people can change under humane conditions, and he knows how terrible life inside prison can be. I've seen men change in the prison system we have now. We have almost no recidivism.

Q. Despite your humanitarian work with prisoners, Nicaragua's Cardinal, Obando y Bravo, wants you expelled from here. How do you explain that?

The Church is undergoing a purification process. We are suffering through it and growing. I see real hope for the future of the Church.

Cardinal Obando y Bravo has declared war on the Christian community in Nicaragua. Since 1981, coinciding with Reagan's adoption of the Document of Sante Fe–calling for the elimination of the theology of liberation–Obando y Bravo has followed a line of expelling dozens of religious people who work with the poor. Nicaraguan priests and nuns are removed from their parishes, and foreign citizens are forced out of the country. Usually he can accomplish this without question. He merely tells the target's superior that he or she is no longer desired, and the church authorities recall the person. But when the Cardinal tried to do this to me, my Mother Superior went to see him to question him. She asked him to put in writing what I had done wrong. Neither verbally nor in writing did he show any reasons. I am still here.

Q. What is your current lifestyle like?

Oh, I have had good health. I've had hepatitis and pneumonia but overcame them. My thinness is due to a degenerative disease. It doesn't bother me. I feel very grateful for these years here. I have learned so much and been encouraged by the courage of the people.

Q. What do you see for Nicaragua's future?

I had a happy youth, but what of Nicaragua's youth. They have suffered and witnessed such pain. The torture is horrible, and it still goes on. The same people funded by the same U.S. system killing people in the same agonizing ways. Can the youth absorb the horror? The war is worse now than during the insurrections. It is prolonged and people are tired. And the worst is yet to come.

Gary Ruchwarger

Gary Ruchwarger
Let Us Do It, Too

When I first met Gary, kids were hanging onto his arms and legs. It was Children's Day in Nicaragua and the youngsters were tugging at big, brown-eyed Gary, urging him to hit the piñata. Hugo Saenz stepped in with a blindfold, and soon Gary was swinging at the candy-stuffed papier-mâché *monster. Screaming and yelling, sticky-fingered children crowded together in the dirt space in front of the wood-slab, concrete - block-bottom communal house of the 6,000-person barrio, Georgino Andrade, what Managuans call a basic proletarian community. Its squatter residents are carpenters, masons, mechanics, electricians, shoemakers, bakers, factory workers, seamstresses, housekeepers, and, like Saenz, the 48-year-old coordinator of the neighborhood association, jewelers. Time soon came for Gary's special announcement. He had painstakingly prepared a speech the night before.*

"There is a saying in Nicaragua that the children are *los mimados* (the pampered ones) of the Revolution, because the main goal of this revolution is to eradicate a system that fomented misery and unhappiness among the children.

"During Somoza's days, the children were hungry, ill, ignorant, exploited. Most were forced to work instead of attending school just so their families could eke out a meager existence. Meanwhile, infant mortality took 120 of every 1,000 lives (today the ratio is 74 to 1,000); malnutrition for children under six was at 68 percent. There was no prevention for polio, measles, tetanus, malaria, diarrhea...

"Nicaraguans are people in love with their children and don't want any more hunger, illness, and ignorance. When

147

Nicaraguans shout the slogan: WE WON, WE ARE FREE, WE WILL NEVER BE SLAVES AGAIN, they say this above all for the children. Today, the most preventable diseases are gone; children can read and write and attend school free, under the law, for at least six years. Today, 67,000 children are in preschools, and there are 70 child development centers. And today, I want to announce that we are going to start the construction of a new child development center in this humble barrio, which is named after the first martyr of the literacy campaign, Georgino Andrade.

"When I returned last to California, where I live, the response was magnificent. I got piles of green bills for the construction of a new center for the "pampered ones." The dollars come from individuals and groups, church people and political activists. And they donated books, toys, puppets, dolls.

"You know already that in Nicaragua there are a lot of foreigners—internationalists—who have what is called "temporary residency." Although our residency is temporary, our commitment to the revolution is not temporary; it is permanent."

(When the applause died down, adults hugged Gary and slapped him forcefully on any spot they found. He was proclaimed an honorary member of the barrio's CDS executive committee. Someone brought him rum and slices of lime, but he didn't sit long before kids led him to the sack races, then the spoon-in-the-mouth run, and other "kids" games. A year before, the northern city of Estelí's branch of the national women's organization, AMNLAE, also approved of Gary's work with them so much that they named him an honorary member. Hugo Seanz says of Gary, "He is popular because he is not pretentious, and is an internationalist who does what he says."

Gary Ruchwarger was born in 1949 in Maryland, the son of Russian Jews. His father, a medical doctor, and mother met in an Italian concentration camp during World War II. Liberated by allied forces, they sailed to the United States, where they were once again confined, this time to a refugee camp until the war ended. In 1970, Gary moved to Berkeley, California to attend the University of California, acquiring both bachelor and masters degrees in history.)

I wasn't political. I was just enough of a liberal to be upset when I started working in the university's financial office and saw students from poor families unable to get loans for their studies. I began asking questions: how can this society be so rich and yet not provide good schooling for its citizens; why should there be poor to begin with?

I also started following national liberation efforts in Third World nations, a logical expression of what I saw in ghettos and barrios of the United States. Nicaragua caught my attention when a commando unit of the FSLN seized the national palace in August 1978. After the victory, the flexible policies of the new government intrigued me, and I joined a tour of the new nation in 1980. I was deeply impressed with what I saw. The hard working people and the CDS fascinated me most. I wanted to study the grass roots democratic movement, so after a revisit in 1981, I got a job with the Ministry of Education teaching.

Teaching English at a Jesuit-run high school in Managua was exciting and exasperating. The school system had inherited real discipline problems. Many students lacked a serious interest in studying and I was tested all the time. My Spanish wasn't too hot and I was a foreigner. Discipline did improve, though, the longer I stuck it out. Not all the students supported the revolution, not by a long shot. Some of the more wealthy teenagers were even oppressive in their opposition to the revolution. Sometimes they tried to provoke incidents by drawing swastikas on their papers, tearing down FSLN signs at school and writing Long Live Pastora on walls. I was impressed at how careful the FSLN younsters were by refusing to fight with the conservatives. They far outnumbered the opponents, and they had the nation's morality on their side, but they did not want to fall into any provocation trap. They even warned me to be careful of the right-wing. One rich parent complained to the school's principal, contending I was a "commie" because I used a pamphlet supportive of the Sandinista revolution as a text.

149

The principal told the parent he had the option of taking his child to another school.

School problems were enough for me then. I wasn't really prepared for the day-to-day living hardships. I was used to comfortable surroundings and gaining things easily. In Managua, everything comes hard. Transportation is a hassle, finding a place to live worse. I had to move so many times, a temporary room here, a partial room there. Getting residency was a real headache, too. The paperwork requirements were always changing. One clerk would tell me one thing, the next another thing. Finally, I went directly to the Minister of Education, Dr. Carlos Tunnerman (currently ambassador to the United States). Even then it took him two personally written letters to nudge immigration to hand over my residency papers. I must say, I could write a thick pamphlet on "How to Get Residency Papers." In 1983, I decided to write a book about popular participation in the revolution, the relationship between the FSLN, the government and the mass organizations. The main mass organizations are: CDS (Sandinista Defense Commitee), JS (Sandinista Youth), CST (Sandinista Workers Committee), ATC (Farm Workers Association), UNAG (National Union of Farmers and Ranchers), and AMNLAE (Luisa Amanda Espinosa Nicaraguan Women's Association).

Nicaragua's grass roots democracy is unique. In Cuba, for example, mass organizations first developed after the triumph and on a top-down basis. But here, the mass organizations began *during* the insurrection and were created from the ground level, often spontaneous groundswells of people just taking responsibility. I chose the Georgino Andrade barrio to study because it is a classic example of how communities have sprouted up. The Ministry of Housing is building homes as fast as it can, hundreds of tracts, but it can't possibly build enough. They estimate it would take 80 years just to keep up with population explosion and to house those displaced from the 1972 earthquake. So after the triumph, whole groups of marginalized unemployed and poor workers squatted on unused land, often owned by rich men who did nothing with it.

People built and still build homes out of whatever they can find. After the communities are begun, government agencies offer basic infrastructure: running water and, usually, electricity, taking neither rent nor taxes, and giving out land titles. At many barrios, like this one, people often don't even pay for water and electricity, as no one from "downtown" comes out to check.

In just three years, this barrio has built 1,100 new homes, many with gardens of flowers, fruit trees and vegetables. Children make up half the residents, and they attend schools newly built. But they lack preschool centers. In 1984, barrio leaders asked me to help raise funds for a new preschool.

Q. What does your study conclude about socialism in Nicaragua?

My book is tentatively entitled, *People In Power: Forging a Grassroots Democracy in Nicaragua.* Based on my 18-month research, I can say that Nicaragua is definitely not a socialist society, but it is a basically democratic one. It offers a "third choice" to poor nations, especially those with strong religious roots. I judge this revolution by how the ruling FSLN encourages the creation of mass organizations, their genuine growth and power to exercise autonomy. I have found that grass roots groups often have more influence on the revolution's direction than do government leaders and agencies. The mass organizations are semi-autonomous from their vanguard party, the FSLN. They have separate structures and funds, sometimes choosing different priorities, and even lobby against some FSLN positions. For example, in 1983, the FSLN proposed a new military draft law calling for compulsory military service for men only. AMNLAE challenged this position, arguing that women were already fighting to defend Nicaragua's sovereignty and should also be drafted. Most men and many women disagree with AMNLAE. A compromise was reached. Women can volunteer for the army, and thousands have done so since the draft was initiated.

One of the most important features of the democratic process is the system of advisors in every ministry and institution of power. The mass organizations have representatives sitting on their executive boards. When grass roots spokespersons complain that a ministry official is not doing his/her job, the complaint is investigated and sometimes the person responsible for negligence or corruption is removed from office. The system is also followed on the grass roots organizational level. Since all leaders are elected they can also be recalled. Individual CDS leaders have sometimes been accused of giving favors to revolutionary supporters and withholding rations to basic goods from others, or of taking bribes. At Georgino Andrade barrio, for instance, some of its leaders were collecting small bribes for writing letters for services that every community resident is entitled to. They were denounced at public assemblies and replaced in new elections. Not since then, two years ago, has this barrio had a reoccurrence of abuse of power. Periodically, one hears or reads a speech by a commandante deploring similar petty abuses of power. A few CDS leaders are ardent supporters of the revolution who slip morally with their new found authority, and others are carry-over hustlers who once cheered Somoza.

Q. What do you think of Marxism?

I am not a Marxist. I think Marxists have made too many errors and ignored too many important questions and sectors of society, such as human psychology and feminism. I believe that FSLN is on the right track and is the best united political party in any nation witnessing liberation struggles. I think, however, that the party is too uncritical of Soviet foreign policy. I believe that what the workers are fighting for in Poland is more compatible with the reality of Nicaragua's revolution than with the FSLN political position on Poland. It is the sad reality of economic and defense needs that seems to lead to such contradictions, which probably also explains why the Sandinista government trades uncritically with Iran. I also think FSLN members have a limited knowledge of socialist development in the world, but there is a real broad sense of justice throughout the party, and the majority of people are exercising power. There is no doubt, for example, that the FSLN won the elections in a fair manner. The right-wing knew the election campaign was honest and that the people would reject them That is why the sector aligned with Reagan's regime declined to run.

Q. How has Nicaragua affected your life?

Nicaragua has changed my life drastically. I've learned to appreciate a whole new way of thinking. A family I lived with was proud to have me know that one family member died fighting U.S. marines in Sandino's days. Their home also served as a safehouse for guerrillas in the 1970s. They are so proud the world is studying *them*, Sandino's Nicaragua.

These people have a solid sense of community, something the vast majority of Americans lack. So many of us live lives of despair and impotence. Here, one is alive with a sense of purpose. I am so moved, I even try to influence visiting U.S. congressmen, but they usually only want to speak with well-heeled opposition leaders.

I miss Nicaragua when I am away, but cultural differences are such that I never feel completely at home here. Then again, I never feel completely at home in the U.S. either. I guess I must accept permanent marginality.

Q. What would you do if the U.S. invades Nicaragua?

If I were in the U.S. when it happened, I'd go crazy. If I am here, I'd be more at ease among friends, and I'd help in civil defense work. I can envision thousands of U.S. citizens coming in Witness for Peace bridages. There may even be a new Abraham Lincoln brigade, but this time they'd be fighting directly against their own government's military. There will also be millions doing solidarity work in the States, tens of thousands in civil disobedience activities. Reagan will not have as easy a go of it as did his predecessors in the Vietnam War. I hope everybody opposed to this war simply goes on an indefinate general strike until the U.S. stops. Such an action started the insurrection in Nicaragua. Now we have that example, let us do it, too.

Other Yankee Sandinistas
The New International Brigades

International solidarity motivates people to travel to Nicaragua to pick coffee and cotton, to construct homes. It is the same spirit that moved people to form the Hands Off Nicaragua Committee during the liberation movement to eject invading U.S. marines in the 1930's and that later organized the Hands Off Cuba Committee and the Venceremos Brigade to help Cuba survive U.S. intervention. Nicaragua attracts brigadistas more interested in stopping U.S. intervention than in prosletyzing for alternative economic-political systems. These Americans are far from dogmatic.

Internationalists began arriving in Nicaragua in March 1980 to help with the literacy campaign. Since then most of the foreign volunteers from the Americas and Europe come for a period of weeks or months to carry out specific tasks, such as building schools, clinics, bridges, or harvest crops. Typical groups from the U.S. include the Boston Brigade of 30 university teachers and students who picked cotton; the Marvin José Lopez North American International Brigade of 52 reforesters who came to carry on volunteer work of the Nicaraguan Lopez, murdered while planting trees; and Operation California, a group of California doctors who worked in rural clinics.

During the harvest season (November-March of each year), hundreds of U.S. citizens work for weeks. The CNSP (Nicaraguan Committee of Peoples Solidarity) says over 3,000 have helped in the past three to four years, while other thousands have arrived from Europe to work in such brigades. A few of the brigadistas stay on, or return to work for longer periods.

No one knows exact figures but internationalists from scores of lands immigrate to work in the new Nicaragua. The number most bantered about in 1984 was 6,000 internationalists, mostly from other Latin nations, Europe and the United States. In other years, there have been more or less. It is widely held that Cuba has sent some 2,000 doctors, nurses and teachers, plus a number of military advisors. Other nations allied with the Soviet Union have also set technicians and advisors. But these men and women serve for a tour of duty, one or two years, and then return, usually well paid, to their nation of origin. It is mostly "Yankees," Latins and a few western Europeans who come to stay. Some of the Latins are exiles or refugees from dictatorships, some are individual experts who help a particular project. Many internationalists from the United States are attracted to see for themselves what the revolution is about. Having seen, they decide to stay, offering skills and solidarity. The U.S. State Department says some 2,500 U.S. citizens live in Nicaragua, but the local U.S. Embassy officials put the figure much lower, at around 700 to 1,000, and of them 150 are Embassy personnel. Estimates of U.S. citizen-internationalist, working and living in the revolutionary process, vary from 300 to 700.

Ann Lifflander, a young Manhattan internist, came to visit Nicaragua and decided to stay.

"I work here because I want to practice medicine where there is support from the government for decent health care. I worked three years in the South Bronx. Each year, our staff was cut, our budget reduced, services and medicines diminished. U.S. public health clinics are not getting sufficient fundings or staff. I want to apply good quality care for poor people and have that appreciated by society. That is Nicaragua," Ann says.

Ann works in a Managua hospital practicing general and internal surgery. She attends to patients and is in charge of half a medical ward, supervising residents and interns, and teaching medical students. She knows that the medicine shortage in Nicaragua, unlike her own nation, is not caused by government or private enterprise, but rather is a by-product of her nation's aggression.

"There are times when patients die because we don't have the medications we need. There are times when we use medication that is dangerous because we don't have anything that is safer. It is the most awful feeling to be taking care of patients, knowing exactly what they need and know that there just isn't any. One reason is sabotage. For example, a pharmaceutical shipload of products was destroyed while en route in Miami. Some people opened all the boxes and wrote 'Death to the Revolution.' Whoever works in customs in Miami is responsible for destroying those donations from Scandinavia. It makes me sick."

Pat Hynds, a former resident of San Fernando Valley, the sprawling Los Angeles suburb, and a graduate of California State University at Northridge, is the mother of three children sufficiently grown to be left behind while their mother devotes herself to the Jesuit-sponsored Central American Historical Institute in Nicaragua.

We American internationalists are not traditional political activists," Pat says, "let alone the Marxists and anarchists who fought for Spain in the 1930's. We are a new model, not entirely in any camp. Whether political, religious or not, we all work for reconstructing this torn nation and keeping the United States' military hands off.

Pat used to teach school in the San Fernando Valley before "the churning inside me, urging me to work for justice, led me to Nicaragua where the majority of people know that the earth was created with enough material goods so that everybody can live a dignified life, and know that if that is not happening it is not because God wants people to be poor but because human beings have set up structures that don't bring that about."

Pat started a newsletter about events and developments taking place in the church, in the indigenous areas of the Atlantic Coast, in the mass organizations, the work places, the diverse political parties, and the war of agression and counter-revolution. Envio, *as it is called, was printed by three people. Now a staff of 20 puts out editions in English, Spanish, German, and French, reaching several thousands around the globe.*
Pat says she will stay in Nicaragua indefinitely.

"In Nicaragua, I count. Here we are choosing life, only that, really. To let life leak out, to let it wear away by the mere passage of time, is to withhold life."

Another American woman who visited and decided to work directly with the revolution is Lisa Rosenthal. Like Pat Hynds, Lisa is also from the San Fernando Valley. She once studied dance alongside Jane Fonda, and later opened her own dance studio school.

"My 'Limber Yard' did well for three years until Fonda unintentionally drove me out of business when she opened her own school," Lisa told me without malice.

"I started taking classes at Valley Junior College. My political science teacher, Farrel Broslovsky, whose writings debunked the myth of Jewish 'persecution' in the Sandinista revolution, put things in perspective for me. I learned that it was not me who is insane but that society is wrong. When I started working for a better society that's when I started to be happy. I was able to step outside myself, and not be so preoccupied with my own ego."

After working in solidarity committees in her area, Lisa made an exploratory trip to Nicaragua and" fell in love with the country's physical beauty, the rich land, the large campesino population so energetically immersed in tilling their own land for the first time in their history. I returned to Los Angeles convinced that American farmers had to see the real agriculture. I wanted to dispel the myth that the state is totalitarian and is usurping private land."

In cooperation with the Matagalpa area Ministry of Agriculture, Lisa organized a tour of Nicaraguan representatives of both private and state farms to meet farmers in the U.S. Daniel Nuñez, a major grower who turned his land over to the cooperative farmers and became the president of the private farmers association, UNAG, spoke in Visalia, California to landowners and producers. In Sacramento, Samuel Amador, Nicaragua's largest private rice grower, spoke with large landowners. They asked pointed questions about alleged communism and totalitarianism in Nicaragua. Amador showed them his checkbook, indicating his commitment to making a good profit with supporting the revolution. Californian and New York agribusinessmen, many of them Reagan supporters, invited them for return visits.

Lisa was effective, productive. She was invited to work with the Ministry of Agriculture in Matagalpa province. During a two-day tour of farms stretched across lush green valleys and stark hanging-cliff mountains, she told me what problems she encounters in Nicaragua.

"Reagan's 'brothers,' the contras, are killing private farmers and some are getting scared, and are worried about participating in production. The contras can't ideologically offer any better deal to farmers than what the revolution has accomplished, so they terrorize them. Twelve million acres of arable land have been turned over to farmers, most of whom never had land before. This land was Somoza owned, or owned by his top supporters, who have since fled. The eventual goal of the revolution is to bring 50 percent of the land under cooperative management, one-quarter state farms, and the remaining quarter in larger private holdings. The agrarian reform laws guarantee that all farmers can keep their lands as long as they produce.

"Another problem for production, is the economic blockade. It affects our cattle's health. So, I am working on raising donations of medicine for blood and skin diseases. A new source of aid may be Israel. Because of its government's policies of aiding U.S. imperialist interests in Central America, several Israeli citizens have started a people's support group called 'In Solidarity with Nicaragua.' I visited Israel recently and saw the enthusiastic people on kibbutz farms. They are much like the thousands of cooperatives sprouting up here. We are working on sending agricultural experts to Israel to study their system."

Lisa switched from the Ministry of Agriculture to work for UNAG in international relations. She organized the first tour of U.S. farmers to Nicaragua. The group of 18 from California, Wisconsin, and South Carolina arrived in time for the 1984 election campaign and for UNAG's first national rally, which drew 25-30,000 of the nation's agricultural producers to Managua. One of the delegates, a young dairy farmer from Wisconsin, Craig Adams, was invited to speak on the same platform with Nuñez and Nicaragua's president, Daniel Ortega. His words were met with roaring applause:

> "Many producers in the United States feel Reagan does not represent us. His government's policies push us off our lands, just as his policies seek to push you farmers off yours, and destroy your great revolution. As United States producers, we are here to say your fight is our fight. We farmers want peace."

Daniel Nuñez and Samuel Amador were both elected to the new 96-person legislature, as part of the FSLN ticket of 61 successful candidates. They invited the U.S. farmers on a tour of farm country in the north. On the air-conditioned bus, I had an opportunity to speak with Amador. His private land is worked by nearly 200 permanent wage earners. He lives in a million-dollar, 25-room Italian-furnished house, yet he can't travel to his neighboring countries.

"The contra radio *(installed by the CIA)* in Honduras announces my assassination is forthcoming," says the rich patriot calmly. "It is impossible for me to cross into Honduras or Costa Rica, and even some areas of my own country."

An elderly dairy farm couple from Modesto, California told me they had voted for Reagan in 1980.

"I am still a registered Republican, but I'll not support Reagan anymore," the man says. Instead of trying to put this revolution down, the U.S. ought to be sending help, trading. That's the only way to make friends, the only way to get anything positive accomplished."

Another couple, Jim and Margaret Goff, work at a Protestant center, much like Pat Hynds' Catholic institute. Goff was born and raised in Los Angeles and California's Bay area, where he is still an ordained Presbyterian minister. Jim is also the 68-year-old coordinator of the Committee of U.S. Citizens Living in Nicaragua, a vocal group of 100 members who protest U.S. military intervention in a variety of ways.

A committee brochure reads:
"Our committee was formed because of our strong opposition to the policy of the U.S. toward Nicaragua and its revolution. We think the war against Nicaragua is criminal and hypocritical. Efforts to promote peace and democracy in Nicaragua, we find, are thwarted because of our government's military actions in Central America.
"On November 25, 1983, we held a vigil for peace at the front gate of the U.S. Embassy in Managua. Since then, we

have held a similar vigil every Thursday morning. Until the U.S. Government develops a constructive rather than destructive policy toward Nicaragua, these weekly visits will continue."

This activity has grown to weekly vigils in several world cities: Los Angeles, Seattle, Philadelphia, New York, London, Paris and beyond. Many hundreds of U.S. citizens have been arrested for practicing civil disobedience in support of Nicaragua.

The Goffs have lived in Latin America for 35 years, and in Nicaragua, four. They are uncertain how long they can continue to work here, but they know, as Jim said, "If it weren't for all us United States citizens running around Nicaragua, it would make the government's war a lot easier."

Ronald Reagan's obsessive efforts to divert attention from the massive electoral victory for the revolutionary FSLN Party resulted in extensive provocations on the very day of Reagan's own election. Sound-barrier-breaking, SR-71 spy jets buzzed Nicaragua's capitol, and war frigates entered close to shore, violating international laws. Scores of members of the U.S. citizens committee, accompanied by Witness for Peace observers, acted to defy U.S. military might. Thirty American antiwar activists spent hours in a small fishing vessel and approached a U.S. war ship "at ready," near the port of Corinto. Shouting, "Leave these waters. We don't need your protection," the Americans shooed the intruder a bit away, temporarily. On shore, over 100 vigil members marched through the streets of Corinto before some of them initiated a two-week vigil, pitching tents near the oil tanks partially destroyed by CIA-organized motor-boat attacks.

Witness for Peace was organized in November 1983, following a cruel attack by contras on a little village in northern Nueva Segovia, called Jalapa. U.S. women, and the Christian group, have maintained a permanent vigil in Nicaragua since. Their message: To conquer Nicaragua, you will have to kill your own citizens.

Witness for Peace volunteers are not "Yankee Sandinistas," in that they do not live or work permanently in

Nicaragua, nor do they have a political program or ideology. They simply seek to stop their government from killing people in yet another land, hoping that another holocaust, such as in Southeast Asia, can be averted.

"We act so that the war is not inevitable," said one vigil member.

The long-term observers learn Spanish before coming for six months or more. By now, members of every race and religion in every state of the union have participated. A U.S.-based staff coordinates efforts and input from 200 supporting groups in Washington, D.C., Durham, North Carolina, and Santa Cruz, California. Jean Abbott, a St. Louis community worker and Catholic, is one of the long-termers, whose tour was nearing an end.

"Americans usually *react* to United States invasions. Here, we have an opportunity to *act* before the invasion," said Abbott, "and maybe, just maybe, help prevent it from happening.

"But whether the American people, as a whole, respond or not, I knew I had to act. And more of us are responding. People who participate are average people, too. Since my stay here, my life has changed to the point that I can say, if the United States government sends a military invasionary force, I'll stay to confront it. None of us wants to die, but if some of us do, I know it will mean a lot. And, by our being here, the U.S. government cannot get away with an invasion like they did in Grenada. Here, there are witnesses."

North American Catholic religious women were among the witnesses to President Reagan's "freedom fighters" slaughter at Ocotal, June 1, 1984. Jean saw the bodies of some of the seven civilians and five military defenders, agonizingly mutilated. She saw the results of damage that caused the infrastructure of the village to collapse.

165

Jean was also at Santa Clara when three teenage girls were shot to death by United States citizens flying United States planes given them by the CIA and the National Guard. Dana Parker, an active-duty national guardsman and police officer in Huntsville, Alabama; James Powell III, a contractor; and another U.S. citizen were spotted by village defenders and shot down just after their Hughes 500 helicopter strafed the girls, who were picking fruit that they would later have sold.

"I sat with Alba Luz' mother and father and we prayed together," Jean recalled. "It was the first time I had ever seen children killed. I was with Alba Luz' cousin, who had been with her when she was shot from above the trees. I could only think that these torturers, these American pilots must have had their feeling side taken away from them. I was so hurt, and then angered. But I didn't get bitter until I saw what the U.S. press did with the 'story.' They totally distorted the reality. They said the girls were killed in battle, ground fighting, they said. There was none. It was a surprise air attack. Alert defenders shot down one of the four attacking planes. The three girls, and one man, were the only victims. I have no idea why the press lies. The children were simply gathering fruit."

After Santa Clara, Witness for Peace and other solidarity workers put together a civil disobedience plan in the event of an invasion. When the signal is given, people from every state will gather at a previously designated church to receive and share information and pray. A nonviolent vigil will be established at congressional field offices of each senator and representative. Each office will be occupied until that congressperson votes to end the invasion. People will converge on Washington, D.C. to engage in nonviolent civil disobedience at the White House. The U.S. citizens in Nicaragua will launch their own plan of action in Nicaragua and, if possible, other U.S. citizens will join them in Nicaragua.

Since the civil disobedience plan was agreed upon, White House intransigence to accept Nicaragua's political reality has motivated some 100,000 U.S. citizens (1986 figures) to pledge they will carry out civil disobedience in the event of an invasion. Some are getting a headstart, hoping to prevent an invasion.

Witness for Peace activists became effective and bold enough by the summer of 1985 that 29 of them sailed into contra-invested waters on the Río San Juan, dividing Nicaragua and Costa Rica. They sought to counter U.S. efforts to topple the elected government of Nicaragua. A band of contras kidnapped them, and accompanying journalists, firing off threatening shots. Although they were threatened with death, the contras released them after a day. An 80-year-old woman and a six-month-old baby were among those captured and shown U.S.-manufactured equipment by the attackers, who said they were followers of Edén Pastora.

Other U.S. citizens living in Nicaragua have also faced attacks by contras. Michelle Costa, a former California health care worker, is one of them. She runs a Spanish language school in Estelí, mainly for visitors and witnesses from the U.S. The New Institute of Central America (known as NICA, is Nicaragua's second Spanish language school for foreigners. The other is located near a city lake in Managua.

NICA was initiated by three women from the U.S., in May 1983. Beverly Treumann, who was a literacy teacher in 1980, Jo Ann Sunshower, and Rose Marie Cardillicchio, are all now part of the U.S. solidarity network. NICA has a Boston office where people register, paying $1,000 a week for the five-week course, including instructions four hours a day, room and board with a Nicaraguan family, community and work experience, and trips. In the first year of operation, 200 people graduated.

"We have 35 students now and ten Nicaraguan teachers," Michelle told me as we squatted under stadium bleachers, waiting out the pouring rain.

"We should graduate twice as many this year, the war permitting," a qualification frequently heard from project chiefs.

The war is quite real to Michelle. NICA's last two closing ceremonies in 1984 had to be cancelled due to contra attacks within close range of the school.

"Three hundred people came to the women's building for our ceremonial party. Suddenly we heard the roar of helicopters landing. A *compa* (short for compañero, or companion-comrade) rushed in, and asked us to participate in aiding the wounded. The contras had just destroyed a coffee plantation and a food storage supply house. They killed, wounded, raped, and kidnapped scores of youths and women. That was our May class farewell.

A subsequent graduating class joined with the townspeople in donated blood when a nearby potato project, supported by the Dutch government, was destroyed. Ten people were killed, including Estelí's chief of police.

"We helped sew up the wounded," Michelle remembers. "One man kept repeating to me, 'We want peace.' Later, a sound truck announced across town that U.S. citizens had donated their blood to heal the workers wounded by their government's bullets. How dare they kill in our name!"

Language school students pick coffee berries at nearby farms as part of their education.

"Picking coffee is an extremely humbling experience," says Michelle. "My first time, I slept on a dirt floor on top of a wooden plank. We ate rice and beans, and retired before nightfall as there were no lights. One day, we heard gunfire around us. We put down our berry baskets and silently walked out of the fields, as our Nica friends grabbed weapons. When the firing died down, the farmer standing next to me said, 'I have my own land now. All I want is to keep it in peace.' Here he is, a Nicaraguan farmer under attack by *my* government, protecting me against possible death by *my* government."

UNIONS IN NUMBERS

CENTRAL ORGANIZATION AND YEAR FORMED	NO. OF UNIONS OR LOCALS	MEMBERSHIP	POLITICAL AFFILIATION
Sandinista Workers Federation (CST) 1979	504	111,498	FSLN
Farmworkers Association (ATC) 1978	480	42,000	FSLN
Health Workers Federation (FETSALUD)	39	15,613	FSLN
Independent General Labor Federation (CGTI) 1963	19	17,177	Socialist Party
Trade Union Action and Unity Federation (CAUS) 1973	15	1,939	Communist Party
Workers Front (FO) 1974	not released	2,000	Marxist-Leninist Popular Action
Confederation of Trade Union Unification (CUS) 1972	17	1,670	Democratic Coordinating
Workers Confederation of Nicaragua (CTN) 1972	21	2,734	Social Christian Party
Nicaraguan Teachers Association (ANDEN)	1	16,000	FSLN
National Employees Union (UNE)	1	17,000	FSLN
Nicaraguan Journalists Union (UPN)	1	300	FSLN
Total:	1,099	227,931	

During the dictatorship there were 133 unions with 27,000 members and 161 contracts signed. Now there are 1,099 unions with 227,931 members who have negotiated over 1,000 contracts, benefitting nearly 292,000 workers. For the first time in Nicaragua's history, agricultural workers, fishermen, miners, and domestic workers have been organized.*

The above data came from a variety of sources: *Envio* of May 1984, *Barricada International* of February 7, 1985, The Ministry of Labor, religious monitoring organizations, and several of the unions and political parties.

*The above data came from a variety of sources: *Envio* of May 1984, *Barricada International* of February 7, 1985, The Ministry of Labor, religious monitoring organizations, and several of the unions and political parties.

1855: The invasion by Bryon Cole and William Walker's soldiers-of-fortune at a time of rift between rulers. Walker wanted to annex all of Central America to the United States. A prominent slaveholder himself, he declared himself president in 1856 and instituted slavery in Nicaragua. President Pierce backed Walker's presidency and sent a U.S. minister to notify Walker that "the Department of State, and especially President Pierce, wished to establish relations with his Government which of course enjoys recognition." Another noteworthy American captain-of-industry, Cornelius Vanderbilt, who enjoyed concessions for shipping lines in Nicaragua, opposed Walker and gave money for his overthrow. Walker was forced to surrender in 1857, but he returned twice again until the British captured him in 1860 and allowed him to be executed in Honduras.

1867: The U.S. affirmed its "protectorate" over Nicaragua mediated by the Dickinson-Avon treaty, which gave the U.S. the right to construct an interoceanic canal.

1896: U.S. military forces land at the Port of Corinto.

1900: The U.S. imposes on Nicaragua and Costa Rica the Hay - Corea and Hay-Calvo treaties in order to acquire eminent domain over the canal route across the Central American Isthmus.

1909: The U.S. intervenes in order to overthrow the government of General José Santos Zelaya using the "Knox memorandum."

1911: U.S. Marines land again at Corinto. They impeach both Nicaragua's and Honduras' presidents and oblige Nicaragua and Costa Rica to accept heavy debt consolidations and new tariffs.

1912: The marines land in Honduras and occupy Nicaragua until 1925. Marines led by then-Major Smedley Butler are responsible for killing General Benjamin Zeledon, on October 4, 1912.

1914: The U.S. imposes the Chamorro-Bryan Treaty, which abolishes Nicaragua's sovereignty, putting political and economic control in Washinton's hands.

1926: The U.S. Marines return after a short respite of some months. This occupation lasts until 1933 when Yankee troops suffered significant losses at the hands of Sandino's guerrillas. In those years, the U.S. organized, trained and equipped a Nicaraguan army, the National Guard, and put Rockefeller Foundation employee Anastasio Somoza Garcia in charge.

1934: Sandino assassinated by the National Guard as he leaves a farewell dinner for the U.S. ambassador.

1954: Nicaragua used as a staging base for CIA organized coup in Guatemala.

1961: The U.S. uses Nicaraguan territory on the Atlantic Coast to train exile Cubans for an invasion of Cuba, and the CIA provided B-26's which flew from Port Cabezas to attack Cuba.

1965: Nicaragua used as a staging base for the U.S. Marine invasion of the Dominican Republic.

1972: The U.S. affirms the Saccio-Vásquez Carrizosa Treaty with Colombia, thus injuring Nicaragua's sovereignty. U.S. armed forces stationed in Panama arrive to protect the Somoza regime after the devastating earthquake.

1978: The U.S. tries to impose a politics of "mediation" in order to preserve the Somoza rule and to interfere with the popular revolutionary movement led by the FSLN.

1979: The U.S. appeals to the OAS for the military intervention of Nicaragua in order to prevent the popular revolution from succeeding. It hoped to use Central American armies the CIA had previously organized in the Condeca. U. S. helicopters landed in Costa Rica. But the OAS refused to play ball. After the July 1979 revolutionary triumph, the counter-revolution begins with Somoza troops who flee to Guatemala, Honduras and Florida. The U.S. assists the contras.

1981: The U.S. officially pays for the counter-revolution, with the CIA in charge of training and equipping contras. The U.S. begins landing helicopters, jets and military supplies in Honduras and El Salvador. Military maneuvers in Honduras begin and continue almost constantly. Honduras becomes a major base for U.S. military operations including the construction of several airfields.

1982: U.S. Ambassador to Honduras, John Negroponte, tells independent congressional delegation that the Boland Amendment, specifically prohibiting funds to overthrow the Nicaraguan government, is merely "a legal formality."

1983: Reagan sends warships to both the East and West Coasts of Nicaragua. First such manuevers in 40 years. Full blockade considered. On October 10, a contra speedboat attacks the Port of Corinto, setting one of the fuel storage tanks on fire.

1984: Lt. Col. Oliver North, White House liason to the National Security Council, coodinates contra activity with private right wing U.S. support groups in pursuit of the policy of low intensity warfare. CIA mining of Nicaragua's harbors.

1985: Congress approves $27 million in "humanitarian aid" for the contras.

1986: U.S. House of Representatives votes $100 million in aid to the Contras.

APPENDIX III
Selected References

The following list of organizations and reading materials was compiled with the help of The Committee of U.S. Citizens Living in Nicaragua (CUSCLIN). You can write to CUSCLIN for information or speakers: CUSCLIN, Apartado Postal 4110-25, Managua, Nicaragua.

ORGANIZATIONS

Central American Health Rights Committee, P.O. Box 384, Planetarium Station, New York, NY 10024. (415) 433-6057.

Inter-religious Task Force on El Salvador and Central America, 475 Riverside Drive, No. 633, New York, NY 10115. (212) 870-3383.

Madre (Mothers in Solidarity with Central America), 853 Broadway, Rm 905, New York, NY 10003. (212) 777-6470.

National Network in Solidarity with the Nicaraguan People, 2025 Eye Street, N.W., Suite 402, Washington, D.C. 20006. (202) 223-2328.

Nicaragua Exchange, 239 Centre Street, New York, NY 10013.

Nicaragua Interfaith Committee for Action, 942 Market Street, No. 709, San Francisco, CA 94102. (415) 433-6057.

Witness for Peace, Office of U.S. Witness, 515 Broadway, Santa Cruz, CA 95060. (408) 425-3733.

Witness for Peace, P.O. Box 29241, Washington, D.C. 20017.

Witness for Peace, 198 Broadway, New York, NY 10038. (212) 964-6730.

PERIODICALS

Barricada International (Weekly, in English and Spanish), Apartado Postal 576, Managua, Nicaragua.

Central America Report, Religious Task Force on Central America, 1747 Connecticut Avenue, N.W., Washington, D.C. 20009.

Envio (Monthly in English, Spanish, German, and French), Apartado Postal A-194, Managua, Nicaragua.

NACLA (Report on the Americas), 151 West 19th Street, 9th Floor, New York, NY 10011.

BOOKS

And Also Teach Them to Read by Sheryl Hirshon with Judy Butler. Lawrence Hill and Co., Connecticut, 1983.

Carlos, The Dawn Is No Longer Beyond Our Reach by Tomás Borge. New Star Books, Vancouver, 1984.

Contra Terror in Nicaragua by Reed Brody. South End Press, Boston, 1985.

Food and Farming in the New Nicaragua by Joseph Collins. Institute for Food and Development Policy, San Francisco, 1983.

Guerrillas of Peace by Blase Bonpane. South End Press, Boston, 1985.

Nicaragua: The First Five Years, edited by Thomas W. Walker. Praeger, New York, 1983.

The Nicaragua Reader, edited by Peter Rosset and John Vandermeer. Grove Press, New York, 1983.

Sandino by Gregorio Selser. Monthly Review Press, New York, 1981.

Sandino's Daughters by Margaret Randall. New Star Books, Vancouver, 1981.

Triumph of the Revolution: The Sandinista Revolution in Nicaragua by George Black. Zed Press, London, 1981.

Turning the Tide: U.S. Intervention in Central America and the Struggle for Peace by Noam Chomsky. South End Press, Boston, 1985.

OTHER LATIN AMERICAN TITLES
FROM CURBSTONE PRESS

poetry:

DE REPENTE/ALL OF A SUDDEN, Teresa de Jesús
(pseud.), trans. by Maria Proser, Arlene Scully & James Scully.
"Poems written after the 1973 coup in Chile. They contend with its
repercussion; the drama, the distrust, the sense of violation and
spoliage [has] universal impact. Highly recommended."– *Booklist.*
Bilingual edition, 92 pp, $7.50pa, ISBN 0-915306-14-X.

LET'S GO!, Otto René Castillo, trans.by Margaret Randall.
Castillo began to write poetry in 1954 when he was exiled from
Guatemala for the first time. He and his guerrilla group were captured
and executed in 1967. "His language is simple, direct, but never
ordinary. He asks not metaphorical involvement from his readers, but
action."– Margaret Randall.
Bilingual edition, 96 pp, $7.50pa, ISBN 0-915306-44-1

QUECHUA PEOPLES POETRY, trans. by Maria Proser &
James Scully. Songs sung on communal occasions by the Quechua
people living around Cochabamba, Bolivia. "They are sweet, pure,
half-cocked, passionate, filthy, raucous, sexist, irreverent, sly, witty,
subversive, heartbreaking, ingenuous; in short, totally human and
alive."– James Scully.
English edition, 72 pp, $7.50pa, ISBN 0-915306-09-3.

POEMS, Roque Dalton, trans. by Richard Schaaf. Dalton has
become a heroic figure throughout Central America and beyond. Born
in 1935 in El Salvador, he was assassinated in 1975 by a rival paction
of the People's Revolutionary Army. "These poems are alive and
urgent: they are necessary reading."– June Jordan.
English ed, 88pp, $13.50cl, ISBN 0-915306-45-X; $7.50 pa, ISBN 0-915306-43-3

THE EARTH IS A SATELLITE OF THE MOON, Leonel
Rugama, trans. by Sara Miles, Richard Schaaf & Nancy Weisberg.
Nicaragua's most celebrated guerrilla poet, here in a first collection in
English, "shows a poetic range which would be impressive in a writer
far older and a promise made painful by his death. [Of his generation of
poets,] those who survive revere him as the finest."– Village Voice.
Bilingual ed, 144pp, $15.95cl, ISBN 0-915306-54-9; $9.00pa, ISBN 0-915306-50-